# redemption road

# Praise for *Redemption Road*

*"If you want to know what it is like to set out on a journey of bereavement, if you want to know how suicide affects a person, if you want to know what it feels like to find some healing, then this is the book for you. Brendan writes beautifully and evocatively about his brother Donal and the lengths that he goes to (the end of the world) for him. I couldn't recommend it highly enough."*
—Paul Kelly, CEO and founder of Console

*"Brendan McManus's profoundly moving memoir of his journey to wholeness and healing after his brother's suicide is a standout. He takes the reader along on a physical pilgrimage, but also on a remarkable journey of reconciliation, grace, and ultimately, peace.* Redemption Road *moved me deeply, and I'm proud of my brother Jesuit for sharing with us his honest and heartfelt story."*
—James Martin, SJ, Jesuit priest, editor of *America* magazine, and author of several award-winning books

*"Brendan McManus has written a very vivid and absorbing account of his personal pilgrimage on the Camino to Santiago de Compostela. Riveting and intense, this is no walk in the park, but an invitation to see Ignatian discernment in action and to accompany a grieving man going through great darkness to light. It is a great read."*
—Fr. William A. Barry, SJ, distinguished spiritual director and author

*"In this beautiful book Brendan McManus shares with us the authentic story of his journey on the Camino. Through his experiences along the ancient route he comes to understand the process of his own transformation as a modern-day pilgrim moving away from despair, searching for the restoration of his faith in hope and love."*
—Dr. Jim Lucey, psychiatrist and medical director of St. Patrick's University Hospital

# redemption road

**FROM GRIEF TO PEACE** through Walking the Camino de Santiago

Brendan McManus, SJ

LOYOLA PRESS.
A JESUIT MINISTRY
Chicago

## LOYOLA PRESS.
### A JESUIT MINISTRY

3441 N. Ashland Avenue
Chicago, Illinois 60657
(800) 621-1008
www.loyolapress.com

Cover art credit: © iStock/rdonar

ISBN-13: 978-0-8294-4411-7
ISBN-10: 0-8294-4411-4
Library of Congress Control Number: 2015959420

Printed in the United States of America.

16 17 18 19 20 21 22 Bang 10 9 8 7 6 5 4 3 2 1

*In memory of Donal;*
*dedicated to my family and*
*all those bereaved by suicide.*


*Even though I walk through the valley of the shadow of death,*
*I will fear no evil, for you are with me . . .*
—Psalm 23 (Donal's favorite Psalm)


*A.M.D.G.*

# Contents

# Foreword

I first met Brendan McManus, SJ, on a November evening in 2007 when I was sharing my personal story with a Console support group of which he was a member. Having lost my own sister to suicide, I set up the suicide-prevention agency Console in 2002 with the desire to support those in a similar situation of loss and hopefully prevent others from dying in such a tragic way. I was impressed by Brendan's authenticity and humility in asking for help, a big challenge, particularly for grieving males. As a priest, Brendan is not afraid to write about his own faith crisis and rage at God, a key theme on this epic journey. Many people will identify with Brendan on the Camino because they will recognize the courageous struggle to keep going, to keep taking the next step, and to keep following the winding trail wherever it takes you.

*Redemption Road* tells Brendan's personal story of walking the Camino de Santiago, some five hundred miles, in memory of his brother Donal, who had died by suicide. It is a story about fraternal love, but also about loss and the quest for inner peace. The enigmatic trail in northern Spain provides the dramatic backdrop for Brendan's healing quest, with its stunning beauty as well as its enormous physical and personal challenges. As a Jesuit, Brendan uses all the wisdom and tools of the society's founder, Ignatius of Loyola, the quintessential journeyman and saint. His sixteenth-century spirituality, with its pilgrim, decision-based approach, guides Brendan through some difficult situations. He learns how to go at his own pace, to be free of the pressure to compete with others, and to "live in the moment," being present to himself and others.

As the founder of Console, I have a keen interest in how people grieve the death of a loved one. In this book, walking is the therapy that allows Brendan to heal the wounds of the past. On the trail he experiences a number of adventures and trials that bring his inner tensions to the surface and pave the way for a deep healing process. *Redemption Road* is a story about redemption, about gently mending a broken life through pilgrimage, movement, and meditation. It is a story about how spirituality is present in the grit of everyday experience, and how a sixteenth-century Basque pilgrim, Ignatius of Loyola, illuminates the journey for us today.

I was particularly moved when Brendan mentions how important Console was for him and how being part of a support group was an essential part of the healing process. What interests me is the uncovering of successful survival skills and creative ways of coping. Here is a book that does precisely that, in a way that is neither preachy nor prescriptive, but convincing because it is personal. I believe there is something unique about the process of suicide bereavement that literally drives people to the End of the Earth (part of the last chapter's title) to seek solace for their wounded souls. I found that Brendan's account beautifully describes the human drive for healing, both its difficulties and its consolations, and culminates in an eminently hopeful conclusion.

Paul Kelly, founder and CEO of Console

# Glossary of Spanish Words

**albergue or refugio**
A very basic and cheap hostel designed for Camino walkers

**Buen Camino**
The greeting given to pilgrims: "Have a great walk"

**café con leche**
Typical sweet Spanish coffee made with milk

**Camino del Norte**
"The Northern Route," the route I walked, following the coast from the French border before heading inland for Santiago

**Camino Francés**
The principal Camino route from Saint-Jean-Pied-de-Port in France, through the Pyrenees and directly west to Santiago

**Camino Primitivo**
The original Camino route, from Oviedo to Santiago

**Compostela**
"Field of stars" is the second part of the city's name, Santiago de Compostela, but it is also the name of the certificate given for finishing the Camino

**credencial**
The special "pilgrim passport" that has to be stamped wherever you stay and is inspected at the end in order to receive the *Compostela*

**El Camino**
The Way, trail, or route; there are many of these pilgrim way-marked routes with yellow arrows, all directing the pilgrims toward Santiago

**etapa**
A stage or section of the Camino linking hostels, around twenty kilometers long; guidebooks outline one stage per day

**flechas amarillas**
Yellow arrows that mark the Camino route

**hospitalero/a**
A volunteer who welcomes pilgrims in certain allied hostels

**menu del día**
A cheap, three-course meal restaurants offer for pilgrims

**peregrino**
"Pilgrim"; the one who walks the Camino

**posada**
Boarding house or small hotel, like a B&B

**Santiago**
"Saint James"; this city is famous for its cathedral, where St. James's remains are reputedly kept, and the destination for all Camino pilgrims

**sello**
"Stamp"; each hostel puts a stamp in the pilgrim passport, which records the progress of the pilgrims

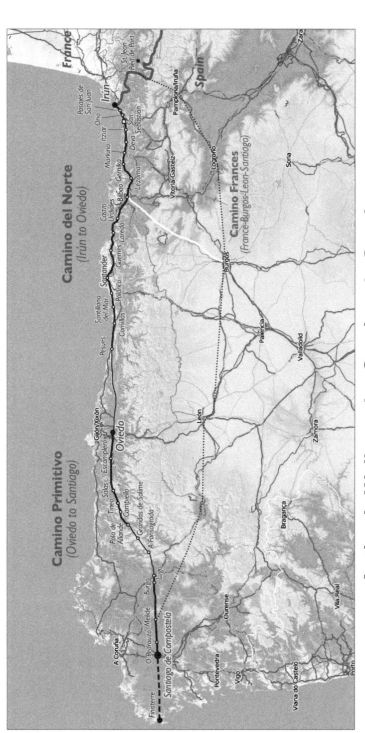

# Author's Walk on the Camino de Santiago
## Camino del Norte • Camino Primitivo

# 1

# Driven by Desire

Driving rain beat off the retreat house window in Connemara, Galway, as I struggled to lead a group of caged teenagers. The lyrics of the Irish band Aslan's song, "How can I protect you in this crazy world?" rang out on the stereo, Christy Dignam's distinctive vocals finding their mark. The song, intended for the teens' spiritual development, cut through to my inner emptiness and sense of guilt. I turned away so they wouldn't see the pain on my face. Despite this, I saw the knowing looks. Irrationally, the song sounded like an accusation: how can you believe after tragedy, especially as a Jesuit priest whose job it is to save people? With the arrival of the bus I was relieved to be finished and out of the spotlight. Numb and churned by unexpected grief, I went through the motions of clearing up.

*I can't keep pretending there is not some wound here*, I thought to myself on the bus into Galway. I was tired of putting on an act, fed up with feeling out of sorts and scraping by in survival mode. I felt of no use to anyone else unless I made the journey into grief myself. The last few years since my brother Donal's[1] death by suicide had been difficult. Physically, the sickness of the soul revealed itself in shingles, depression, and a recurring flu virus. Psychologically, the initial shock, the numbness of the funeral, and the aftershock had been devastating, but now there was the low-grade, ongoing, silent anguish, not to mention the spiritual crisis that I was only dimly aware of.

As with many other grief survivors, life was a continuous battle: presenting a brave face while my insides screamed decay and loss. Many friends, family, and colleagues were magnificent in their concern and support, but I needed a little extra help, so I hesitantly consulted counselors and other healing professionals. Eventually, I found Console, a suicide support group. It was a safe place to be myself, express my feelings, and share with peers who had lived through the same horror. Still, something was left unhealed. I wondered how I could trust in life again and transform this experience of loss into new life and outreach. As a priest with a faith crisis I was living a contradiction: communicating a loving God was challenging. Life had changed dramatically; with suicide the veil had been lifted, and there was no going back to old sureties. I couldn't keep limping along like this for much longer—something radical was required to reawaken my passion and energy.

On that bus journey, the story of the forced convalescence of St. Ignatius of Loyola sprang to mind. The saint was a Basque courtier who founded the Jesuits (my order) almost five hundred years ago. A prototypical psychologist, Ignatius began examining his inner moods and feelings after a cannonball shattered his leg and forced him to spend months in bed. This experience and a subsequent walking pilgrimage were the catalysts for a radical process of transformation. The isolation of his sickbed meant he had to forgo his favorite romantic novels, which were unavailable, for a *Life of Christ* and a book about the saints. He still fantasized about his romantic aspirations, however, and alternated these with the spiritual reading, using his imagination to picture radically different scenarios. In one daydream he would win the hand of a famous lady, while in another he would outdo the saints in fasts and pilgrimages. He made a strange discovery on his sickbed, that while:

> thinking of worldly matters he found much delight, but after growing weary and dismissing them he found that he was dry and unhappy. But when he thought of imitating the saints, he not only found consolation but even afterwards he remained happy and joyful.[2]

The contrasting moods that resulted were deeply significant. Ignatius deduced that God was communicating directly with him, inviting him to reflect and make decisions, and ultimately leading him to a profoundly different life.[3] The heart of his insight was that his superficial desires (self-serving) were not genuinely life-giving and resulted in unhappy, desolating feelings. However, his deepest desires (serving others) were invigorating and rewarding and resulted in happy and consoling feelings. Illness forced him outward into the joyful challenge of life instead of half-living in a comfortable desolation.

Consolation is an inner movement that stirs up feelings of peace, hope, and love, and orients us toward God and toward helping others. In *Inner Compass*, Margaret Silf writes that consolation is "a signal that our hearts, at least for that moment, are beating in harmony with the heart of God."

Though I knew this story well, what struck me was the way his illness became a crucible for transformation. My own illness and resultant moods seemed to find an echo in Ignatius's experience: the answers could be found through pilgrimage, self-awareness, and reflection.[4] Similarly, I had to choose between different life-giving or deadening alternatives, and this choice led irrevocably to action, a journey, or a quest. As soon as he was well, Ignatius the pilgrim limped his way to Jerusalem and into a new life. Ignatius formulated all his experiential wisdom on moods and decisions into a spiritual manual called the *Spiritual Exercises*,[5] a guide I often use in my work and prayer. Ignatius had known great depression and desolation and had lived through his own "dark night." He had even contemplated suicide once. There was a striking parallel between my own story and desire and St. Ignatius's.

I have a vivid memory of a thirty-day pilgrimage I had done as part of my Jesuit training some twenty years previously in Spain, walking in the actual footsteps of Ignatius, begging for food and lodging.[6] This was one of the defining moments of my vocation, where paradoxically I felt free even though I had nothing, full even though I was hungry, and alive even though I was living a precarious existence. My intuition told me I needed to get back to that primitive aloneness with God, of being on the road, radically open to life. Having tasted that once, I desired it again. At the age of fifty I knew I couldn't go begging, but I could still hike and carry a backpack.

An aficionado of pilgrimages, I was intrigued by the legendary Camino de Santiago and had read extensively about it. I had seen the movie *The Way*,[7] with Martin Sheen, which movingly dealt with grief and loss through walking. The seeds of an idea began germinating in my head: I could walk the ancient route to *Santiago*, searching to recover the "lost passion"[8] and put together the fragments of my life. I welcomed the necessary asceticism, the abandoning of myself to the vagaries of the road, and the creation of silence through the meditative rhythm of walking.

I wanted to listen to my heart, to be in contact with nature, and to live from the deepest part of myself, like Ignatius. I would bring a symbol of my brother to Santiago on behalf of my family. Merely saying the words in conversation, "to walk the *Camino*," produced a visceral change in me,

*What do you long for? What in your heart do you really want?* Ignatius encourages us to examine our desires, pay attention to our feelings, and reflect on what emerges. Only when we discover our deepest desires do we discover God leading within us.

igniting a fire. I took it as confirmation that this was a genuine desire[9] and that somehow my healing was tied to it. The Camino wasn't just a trip or a stroll but a search for spiritual survival, reshaping the broken pieces in some meaningful way. A journey into the unknown, it was simultaneously thrilling and terrifying.

That winter I set about planning the trip, exploring guidebooks, websites, and blogs. I gathered the necessary hiking equipment and began planning for this eight-hundred-kilometer walk. There was a glut of information and advice on the Camino, not all of it coherent. For example, it was confusing that the trail has no fixed starting point but only one destination, and a "pilgrim passport" but no borders. There are, in fact, multiple Caminos to Santiago, not just one, and as many opinions on walking the Camino as there are people—each of whom has a different motivation or philosophy for walking this ancient road.

After much reflection, I decided to walk the Camino de Santiago in this manner:

- I would walk alone as a pilgrim.[10] This was a solo quest, and I wanted time to sort out my head, reflect, and meditate.
- I would walk the less traveled northern route, *Camino del Norte* (not the classic *Camino Francés*), eight hundred kilometers west along the coast from the French border. Though short on infrastructure it was much more scenic.
- As a symbol I would bring Donal's old Barcelona FC T-shirt to place on the altar in Santiago on behalf of my family.
- I would collect sponsorship for the Console suicide-prevention organization in Ireland that I had been involved with.
- My inspiration and guide would be St. Ignatius of Loyola, the walker and pilgrim,[11] using his *Spiritual Exercises* to guide me.

Normally a weekend hiker, I had to do extra training before departing, walking the mountains around the west of Ireland with a pack full of bricks. Packing the night before departure was a frantic back and forth on the bathroom scales to reduce weight. On a drizzly morning in early June I waited on the tarmac at Dublin Airport, my cape pulled around me. I shivered in my light hiking clothes, anticipating Spain's warmer climes. My backpack weighed in at 7.7 kg on the check-in scales, the result of ruthless repacking that meant abandoning my sleeping bag.[12] Still tired from my job, I slept all the way on the plane and stepped out melting in the 77-degree heat of Biarritz, France.

> St. Ignatius often referred to himself as a pilgrim. He understood that his spiritual journey was one of traveling light and being open to God's leadings. This formative experience of interpreting his own experience while traveling through Europe led to him writing *The Spiritual Exercises*, a guide that illuminates our own pilgrimage toward Jesus.

Waiting for the train to Irún, my starting point on the French-Spanish border, I fell in with a seasoned Canadian pilgrim, Jim, who was walking the French route for the tenth time. Though strangers, we quickly became friends, united by our hiking gear and common destination—my first experience of the unique Camino bond. We exchanged stories of what drew us to the Camino. And even though he had more experience, I was immediately struck by his humility, radiating peace, and a willingness to offer advice. We took off in opposite directions; he was for Saint-Jean-Pied-de-Port. I was never to see him again.

As I boarded the local train alone, I felt excited and anxious, imagining myself on the mythical Camino de Santiago the next day. The train jolted to a stop in the French border town of Hendaye, where it awaited a connection. I realized I could save an hour by simply walking three kilometers into Irún in Spain. Slowly and deliberately I hoisted my Camino backpack for the first time and strolled up a non-descript street into Spain's Basque Country. At the border, I paused at the International Bridge of Santiago, a fitting start for my pilgrimage. I made a heartfelt prayer, asking for protection, courage, and health for the next month. It was an anticlimactic start to the Camino. I had anticipated a huge gateway, a crowd of locals, a dramatic feeling, but there was just a tar road, a rusting bridge, and distant terracotta roofs.

The two towns were so intertwined that I was in Irún before I knew it. I approached my first church on the Camino, the imposing seventeenth-century Santa María de Juncal, expecting medieval-style hospitality. I was met with locked doors. Somewhat put out, I composed my pilgrim prayer on the doorstep and then set off to find an *albergue* (a very basic and cheap hostel designed for Camino walkers), which ended up being a cramped double apartment by the railway. It had been some years since I slept in a bunk, so imagine my horror when I realized that there was no door on the rooms, so I would be effectively sharing the space (along with the noises, smells, and cramped quarters) with all thirty occupants. The hostel owner sensed my discomfort—my squeaky-new clothes revealed a greenhorn—and drew me in with a smile. He was extremely helpful in indicating the next day's walk, called an *etapa*, or stage, and showed me where to stay on the map. He gave me my first official stamp (*sello*) in my *credencial* (pilgrim's passport, which is stamped everywhere you stay and inspected at the end to get the *Compostela*, the certificate given for finishing the Camino), which was strangely reassuring, given that this was the beginning of something largely unknown.

I hardly slept with the cold, and regretted leaving the sleeping bag. Not a good start for a thirty-day walking marathon. Getting up at 6:30 a.m. was a shock to the system, and it took me about forty sluggish minutes to get my gear sorted. Once outside, a dappled sunrise dispelled my fears, and, feeling expansive, I took a side trip to Hondarribia to see and taste the ocean. Brightly decorated houses, windows, and doors alerted me to the fact that I was in Basque territory, with its unique colors, spirit, and language. There on the quayside was the dramatic start to the Camino I sought—a huge poem displayed in Basque and Spanish that began:

> The Camino invites, you discover; you can take a detour from it any time you want. It is a way of water and earth that you cross by bridge or boat; it takes you away from the sound of traffic and brings you to the murmur of the river, to the ceaseless movement of tides charged with salty air.[13]

It was a curious, contemplative take on the Camino, yet food for my pilgrim soul.

Unfortunately, I wasn't prepared for the huge hill I encountered rejoining the trail to Guadalupe Sanctuary. Any vestiges of poetry or mystique soon vanished as I perspired up a busy, winding road, a clatter of construction up ahead. I paused a moment to light a candle in the charming chapel at Guadalupe. After a paltry lunch in the car park, as I had forgotten to get provisions, I continued along a charming hillside trail. Its scrub bushes and deep red soil reminded me of hill walks around Dublin. The rest of the afternoon seemed effortless, though the trail was dusty. I was enchanted with the tinkling of cowbells and sharp tang of goats. It augured well for the Camino, if only I could keep grounded in "one step at a time" and walk day by day.

Fourteen kilometers later, I finally arrived in Pasajes de San Juan, a lovely little traditional fishing port cut out of sandstone cliffs. Famished, I had tuna casserole in a café for dinner and then strolled along the dramatic cliff path above a turquoise sea. Eventually I found a sheltered wildflower garden for a siesta while waiting for the hostel to open. On first sight the *Hospital de Peregrinos* was bright and welcoming. The *hospitalero* (hostel manager), Felice, was the perfect host, going to great lengths to make me feel welcome. My bunk was in a spacious and airy loft with only three others—sheer luxury.

Felice took me aside conspiratorially and told me there was one crucial thing about the Camino. It was the first real test of my rusty Spanish. I wondered what he was building up to—some personal safety warning maybe or certain places to avoid. With much gravitas he announced, "To avoid getting lost on the Camino always follow the flechas amarillas [yellow arrows]." He explained: "There are different systems of marking the Way[14] in different regions of northern Spain—shells, arrow posts—but they can mean different things depending on the region. The hand-painted yellow arrows, however, will always point you in the right direction. They will appear every two hundred meters or so; all you have to do is be alert to them." In fact, it was to prove one of the most useful pieces of advice I received and saved a lot of wasted time. Felice (sounding like the Spanish word for "happy," *feliz*) was well named.

Happy that I had not overexerted myself on my first real day of walking, I took a leisurely stroll along the harbor as the sun melted into the sea. Just opposite, I could see the next day's walk, an almost vertical ascent up the craggy hillside. Having gone hungry that day, I remembered to buy ample provisions for the following day's lunch. In the plaza I met two women walkers, one Italian and one Dutch, and we chatted warmly over a drink and some clam chowder. It wasn't long until we got down to business: why we were walking the Camino. This is a common topic among hikers. Protective of my own privacy, I was somewhat vague ("midlife crisis"), but that question would echo in me more and more. Well tired at this stage, I slept in a dreamless bliss, snug under a hostel blanket.

The next day was over before I knew it. Footsore and tired, I limped into Orio in the late afternoon in the company of two Spanish men I had met on the way. I noticed a rhythm developing, even at this early stage: 6:00 a.m. start, walk all morning, make your own lunch, find an albergue before it gets hot, attend a pilgrim Mass in town, and spend a long afternoon reading or reflecting before a cheap *menu del día* meal. The private hostel in Orio was something special, even if it was a bit dearer (€10) than the municipal ones. In the basement of a family home, it was clean and bright with extensive views of endless green hills.

I was coming to know the ecstasies and agonies of the famed Camino del Norte. The steep hills were tough on a hiker, requiring considerable toil and sweat. I had already scaled two substantial mountains in a day and seen the glorious city of San Sebastian and its crescent beaches. It was surreal trekking along the immaculate, deserted city promenades first thing in the morning, trying to find the quirky yellow arrows. However, the real payoff was the views—the sea always in sight, with its soaring cliffs and rising gulls. The places were all distinctly Basque: cryptic road signs, guttural accents, and the architecture. Orio had some lovely sixteenth-century houses with intricate carvings on their sandstone lintels.

Even though I was only three days into the journey, it felt like an eternity—as if I had entered another dimension, where time had slowed and life was different. More and more I savored the morning walks, a meditative invitation to get into a stride and surrender to it. I had not experienced any great insight yet, simply operating on a survival level: eating, walking, drinking, talking, and sleeping. Doing my Review of the Day[15] that night, I was surprised to find that I had been in a positive, upbeat mood all day. Ignatius named this "consolation," and it seemed to confirm my deep desire to be on the Way.

# 2

# An Inner Light

It was wondrous being on the go as the dawn arrived, a golden, ethereal light. I watched the rising sun inhabit the outside landscape, bringing it into being. This transformation evoked an essential reverence as I took to the road. The thrill of anticipating the day ahead overshadowed my corporeal struggle to get moving. Bleary-eyed and muscle-stiff, I soon thawed in the sun's warmth on the main street. In response to nature's solar display, an inner glow kindled in me.

I scuttled across the deserted town's quays, over the river Oria, and into the welcoming woods. The trail's gravel path wound its way under the highway and up a hill. I eased into the walking rhythm in the cool morning air, the only sound the click of my walking poles. Happiness overtook me like a lost friend; I couldn't believe I was fit, healthy. I felt like a medieval pilgrim on a sacred quest to St. James's tomb. A sense of possibility and optimism surged with every step. Santiago seemed like just a few easy days' walk away.

I was thinking about my brother Donal in the halcyon days before "the great sadness." He had been this little cheeky blond-haired tyke who was always getting into trouble. Football mad, he would play for hours at a neighbor's house, his passion and commitment evident even then. Donal was smart and witty as a teenager, and his sense of humor and big broad grin charmed all around him. With a natural ability for analysis and strategy, he excelled at bridge, even winning a congress (a high-level bridge competition) with our father while still a youth. His football exploits saw him play for his club and even as a county minor at Croke Park's hallowed turf in Dublin. He later worked in farming and construction, but very few knew he had a PhD from the University of Ulster. Probably his greatest gift was his compassion for others: Donal gave almost all his money to charity, and he would go to extraordinary lengths to help someone in trouble—he once used the curtains from one of his rental apartments to cover a friend who was homeless. This was a talented, outgoing, sporty man who had a big heart. He was the light of our lives. This was my brother Donal.

High in the hills near the coastal town of Zarautz, the forest cleared, and I entered a wine region. The bright green vines stood out against the dark forest and red soil. Arranged in rows, they were all well-ordered and tended. I met a man coming out of a vineyard, and we fell into conversation. His leathery skin betrayed much time spent outdoors. He carried an old pair of pruning shears and told me he was busy trimming the vines surrounding his property to keep them productive.[16] It reminded me of the penitential aspects of the Camino, the necessary asceticism that is an inevitable part of any courageous endeavor.[17] Living simply and without luxury focuses the mind on deeper values and longer-term spiritual rewards. I felt some benefits in interior freedom, humility, and awareness already. Peering closely at some vines, I could see how pruned bushes were much more productive. I didn't realize how apt this metaphor would be later in the journey.

A descending trail of switchbacks brought me to the sea again at Zarautz. I took some time out on its wonderful promenade to contemplate the waves. Stopping at a local coffee shop for breakfast, the *café con leche* (coffee made with milk) was blissfully sweet, and the croissants filling after a two-hour fast. The sun beamed in through the tinted window, and I felt pleasantly warm and drowsy. Reluctantly I gathered my gear together and asked the way to the Camino. To my surprise, the entire café, with typical Latin enthusiasm, all gave me directions simultaneously and on different routes.

I was back up in the mountains again shortly, surrounded by butterflies and lost in the Zen of walking.[18] I traversed roads, forests, and fields in an ever-changing pastoral landscape. At a mountain crossroads I met an older man with a tracheotomy tube in his neck, and though he had difficulty speaking, he kindly briefed me on the trail ahead. He was at pains to point out the local hermitage that had been damaged by recent roadwork. As I continued, I realized I was in walking heaven: the endless farmland framed by forest was the jewel of Basque Country. At one stage I lay down in an idyllic wildflower meadow for a siesta but woke up covered in bites. Translucent butterflies still surrounded me though.

As I came out of the forest onto a remote paved road, I mistook a house bedecked with soft-drink advertising for a café. Out of water and parched, I knocked urgently on the door and was taken aback to find it was a private house. Laughing at my mistake, the owners graciously filled my water bottle and invited me in. When they learned I was Irish, they insisted that their teenage daughter practice her English with me. I could sense the parents' pride as we conversed briefly. It was a moment I wanted to hold on to forever: a simple human exchange, but significant in that it was pregnant with the hopes and dreams of this Basque family. I was humbled.

Looking at the map, I was thrilled to see I was only fifteen kilometers from the birthplace of my Basque guide and inspiration, Ignatius of Loyola. A huge basilica and Jesuit residence now encompass his family home, the iconic Castle of Loyola.[19] In 1521, during his convalescence experience here, Ignatius woke up to the significance of inner moods and discernment.[20] He subsequently wrote the *Spiritual Exercises* as a guidebook

> While recuperating from a cannonball injury, St. Ignatius noticed that his dreams of pursuing romance and chivalric adventures left him feeling initially excited but ultimately dry and dissatisfied, while his dreams of serving God filled him with hope and a lasting contentment. Through this process of discernment, Ignatius discovered a new life path.

for trainers helping others to have the same enlightenment. The *Exercises* use the analogy of physical exercise, which is useful for getting in shape, fighting flab, and maintaining health, and applies it to spiritual practices that promote integration, freedom, and healing.[21] This process of becoming aware often implies renewal or restoration: bringing light into the darkness of our lives, healing wounds and destructive tendencies.[22]

I could relate to the challenge of finding God in the darkness of my grief experience and the hope of rekindling my inner flame. Likewise Donal, originally a person of light, had been overtaken by the darkness of depression and suicide. Now, in death, I believed that whatever shadow or negativity Donal suffered would be eclipsed by that divine light; he would be restored by God.[23]  The Camino was a "spiritual exercise"—a pilgrimage offered for the good of his soul, I thought, not realizing what was in store for me. Redemption, being restored or healed, was the goal. The Camino provided the ideal way to achieve this: shedding the darkness of unhelpful dependencies,[24] and glimpsing the light of transformation.

The shadows were long when I got to Itziar after twenty-eight kilometers—the furthest I had walked. The heat was fierce in the last climb up to the village, and my legs were spent. Sore and sunburned, dehydrated and out of energy, I was disappointed to find no hostel in the village, and the six kilometers to the next one felt impossible. It was then that I understood the wisdom of planning the walk in stages (*etapas*) so that the hostels were a walkable distance from one another. My guidebook listed a nearby rural hostel that ran a shuttle service, and some kind Spanish pilgrims rang to book a place on my behalf. After an hour's wait, I discovered the owner would only collect groups, so I was stranded. With night approaching, I turned down a lift to the next town as I didn't want to skip a section (how ironic this would be later). Thoroughly beaten, I collapsed into a cheap hotel and an early night. When I reflected on the day, however, I realized it had been rewarding. The beauty of nature and the kindness of strangers predominated. My enduring image was of those luminous butterflies and their whimsical flight.

The next morning I woke up worse for wear, feeling my age and the sting of lactic acid in my muscles. I could hardly get out of bed, and the euphoria of the previous day rapidly dissipated. Feeling I had overstretched myself, I decided to be more moderate in my planning. I still felt a bit foolish for not making it to a hostel, but I wasn't going to beat myself up about it as I was still learning the ropes. Determined to walk within my own limits, I resolved not to be dictated to by the guidebook, other walkers, or circumstances.[25] Too much of

---

One of the key principles of Ignatian spirituality is detachment, a process of letting go of unhealthy attachments to find balance. We may need to let go of

- expectations,
- addictions,
- bad relationships,
- a grudge,
- an unsatisfying job,
- certain habits, or
- possessions.

Detachment helps us be truly free, to choose God's path and to grow closer to God.

my life had been spent ignoring my body and my instincts, and I had paid the price. Fortunately I had an extra week in hand, just in case I needed more time. Backpack on, I stepped outside from the tranquil comfort into a flurry of wind and rain. *How could two days be so different?* I wondered. *How could I feel so reluctant and fatigued now?*

The first time I saw Adrian walking toward me, he looked like he had been through the wars, with trousers muddied to the knees and a cape flying in the wind. He was thin and wiry, just over sixty years old, and very focused and determined. We fell in together. Initially it was a struggle to understand each other, but I did pick up that he was Dutch, retired, and also walking alone. He couldn't believe I was only getting started midmorning and that I was taking it easy. My explanation that I had made a mistake with the stages and had to get in sync didn't impress him. We stopped to take off our rain gear, but the rain restarted. As we walked down a steep concrete lane greasy with runoff, Adrian started to slip, and the next thing I knew, my feet were going from under me too. We ended up walking on the narrow grass verge for safety, relishing our shrewd escape. It started to rain again, and out came the waterproof gear—it was a tedious process we had to repeat often. Within an hour we arrived in the quirky town of Deva,[26] our destination.

Adrian and I had to take a special elevator down the hillside to the town center since it was so steep. In the elevator we met two locals who insisted on bringing us to the tourist office. After the all-important stamp in our credenciales, they gave us a key to get into the hostel that was located back up on the hill. Walking back, Adrian was delighted to get into the hostel so early, saying, "You are my good luck for today. Five minutes ago we didn't have anything, and now all this." Then he said an even stranger thing: "That is what it is like every day on the Camino; good things just happen." It struck me as true to my own limited experience so far, that when you are open and free, all manner of good things follow. I carefully stored these words in my heart.

The hostel was an old abandoned sports center that smelled damp and of accumulated sweat. Once set up in the hostel, I went for a swim[27] at Lapari Beach, a deserted sandy cove at the mouth of the harbor. In an adventurous mood, I had a look around town, beginning with the sea cliffs and the busy port. I was drawn to the town jewel, the church of Santa María la Real, with its Gothic entrance and fortified facade. Though built in the fifteenth and sixteenth centuries (the time of Ignatius), it was the seventeenth-century baroque altarpiece that drew me to Mass there. Not an expert in church architecture, I have nevertheless been fascinated by how a building reflects the spirit and faith of the time. Designed as a place of encounter between the divine and the human, this largely renaissance space was about order, light, and symmetry. Looking up, I marveled at the ribbed vault, a triumph of uncluttered order, and thought about Ignatius's idea of balance,[28] an ordered life that frees us to be our true selves: a light for the world.[29]

Back in the hostel I had time to reflect on the phenomenon of the Camino after some hard-earned experience. The trail was a cross between extreme hiking, ascending some five hundred meters of altitude every day carrying a backpack, and hosteling, which meant sharing an international communal space for laundry, dinner, and socializing. The beaches and the high passes were magnificent, but you could be forgiven for wondering who designed such a testing route. Without doubt my favorite part of the routine was getting up early, silently slipping out of the hostel, and ambling up a deserted country trail. After that, I just "followed the yellow arrows" as my host Felice in San Juan had said.

The simplicity of life became beguiling, doing ordinary things (eating, sleeping, walking, praying) but with great awareness and presence. The mere motion of walking through Basque valleys and meadows was transformed into prayer and contemplation as I realized I was a creature searching for the Creator. Just as contemplation is a wordless communication with the divine, walking facilitates this process of inner silence and wordless intimacy. I knew well the trap of being stuck "in the head" and falling prey to guilt, remorse, and rumination. Having lived in the shadow of grief and desolation too long, I desperately craved some spiritual renovation. I felt that Ignatius, the archetypal contemplative and pilgrim, would have approved of this freedom quest.[30]

> Just like St. Ignatius, many of us are chained in some way to superficial desires. To achieve genuine freedom, St. Ignatius invites us to face our fears, make discerned decisions, and act against unhealthy attachments. This takes courage, self-awareness, and a radical dependence on God.

The next day I was up first and left the hostel in the dark. My legs felt good, as did my spirits with the help of sleep and rest. The guidebook[31] described the forthcoming day's walk thus:

> This is a beautiful but difficult high level route through some very remote country. It would be unwise to tackle this in bad weather if you were alone or unsure of your capabilities.

I reckon I ticked both those boxes right off. Fortunately, the weather was good and made the going much easier. The morning light shimmered in the trees, and the mist slowly burned off the peaks. The dirt track seemed to wind endlessly up through pine forests and valleys. Early in the day I caught up with a limping Austrian man, but he rejected all attempts at conversation. I met him several times that day, but he never returned a greeting. Coming to understand the need for silence and radical aloneness, I let him be. Alone again, I was wrapped in the stillness of a pine forest for the morning and then a scented eucalyptus one. It was an ecstasy of rural solitude.

Later, I fell in with a group of Italians and one Spaniard whom I could communicate with. I was glad of their company because I was starting to flag, and my right foot was sore. It was getting hot now, and the last downhill section was particularly difficult. I felt like I was being carried by the group, and even though little was said, we had an unspoken camaraderie. We arrived in Markina around 1 p.m. I had intended to walk on to the next village, where the hostel was a monastery, but thought the better of it. I was fairly done in and glad to sit around with the others outside a bar. Adrian was among the group, and while we had not seen each other all day or spoken a word, there was an understanding between us.

The hostel was at the rear of a church, and quite a crowd of pilgrims was waiting. The volunteer hospitaleros arrived late, a real test for all of us who were hot, sweaty, and hungry. It was frustrating waiting for the hostel to open, but cultivating patience was my only option. I had an interesting conversation with an older Spaniard who was doing the route in a camper van. Living the Camino ideal, he lamented the state of the world and the damage caused by individualism and consumerism. He contrasted this with the Camino, where there is so much time to be with yourself and to be conscious of others and the world around you. I knew what he was talking about—on the Way you are outside time, looking in on the world and its crazy ways.

# 3

# Down to the Bone

Unable to sleep, I went down to the front door, where a small group was smoking and relaxing. I quickly realized these were hospitaleros, the volunteers who ran the albergue. I heard them say they were from Barcelona, and just for fun I said I was from there too. This livened things up somewhat, and they all teased me. *Donal would have done the same thing*, I thought, using humor to help break barriers. When the jokes ran out, we moved on to more serious matters, talking about neuro-linguistic programming[32] and other therapies.

To my surprise, one of the women admitted that she needed urgent help with depression and anxiety. A number of others interjected, trying to calm her, but she shrugged them off. She zeroed in on me, asking for specific advice. This was particularly distressing, given Donal's history. I repeated the advice I had given him: "Get good help, get the best professional help, and get it fast." Excusing myself, I left to go to bed. Afterward in my bunk, I found it hard to let go of the woman's dilemma. How had this same issue followed me here to a remote corner of Spain? What did it mean? One thing was certain: the Camino was already challenging me deeply on how free I was of my past. Was this part of a process of stripping away all pretense and having the real me emerge? It was too early to say.

I remembered a morning more than twenty years ago, when I was driving Donal to see a specialist in mood disorders. Very worried, I had taken time off work to try to support my brother. Getting help for him was nerve-racking because it was unfamiliar territory and carried some stigma for both of us. I knew it was difficult for my brother to hand over intimate health secrets to a stranger, not knowing if that would improve things. We met with the doctor, who prescribed some medication, but Donal only temporarily adhered to the regime. In subsequent years he went through the same cycle: getting advice, ignoring it, and gradually deteriorating. I could only look on in dismay. He got progressively worse, and the symptoms became more defined, even though he showed none of this to the world. I could feel him slipping away, and like the rest of my family, I was powerless to help.

As time went on and Donal became more unreachable, my worry intensified, and my attempts to reach him became more futile. As someone whose job is to help people, I found it particularly excruciating to be subjected to a slow, protracted freeze-out and to watch someone I loved disintegrate before my eyes. While much of this was attributable to depression, it was hard not to take it personally or feel some guilt. Loaded with haunting memories, I was distraught to be asked that same question about help for depression. But I knew that the *hospitalera* had to make her own choice to seek help—bitter experience had taught me I couldn't save anyone. I went to sleep.

I left the hostel the next morning in a somber mood, a grey dawn creeping over the Basque countryside. After more than an hour of hard walking, however, I realized I had left my walking poles back at the hostel. Frustrated, I weighed whether to go back and finally decided to walk on, feeling more like a simple pilgrim. Did I really need them after all?

To make matters worse, I lost my way in the hills for more than two hours. I had faithfully followed the yellow arrows up a steep hill and through a small mountain village. Some indistinct arrows took me into an alpine meadow, and I must have missed a turn as I had difficulty following an increasingly faint track. Suddenly I came onto a sheer face surrounded by pine trees. I could see my destination on the next hill dead

> While on his way to Montserrat, Ignatius wanted to avenge a Moor (a Muslim) whom he thought had insulted the Virgin Mary. He couldn't decide whether to kill him, so at a fork in the road, Ignatius let his mule decide. Fortunately, the mule chose the opposite path of the Moor. This decision was clearly not discernment, but may have led Ignatius to find a better way to make decisions later.

ahead, and the desire was to keep going, but there was no way forward. I called out for help several times. No answer. I had to resist the destructive urge to keep pushing forward. This was a time for careful discernment. Ignatius of Loyola is identified with good decision making, but even he had to learn through reflection on bitter experience.[33] His main insight for a good decision was to become free from any undue influence, poised like the midpoint of a balance.[34] Uncovering the biases or sometimes-hidden influences was the real challenge for him as it was for me.

Examining my present situation, I realized I was driven by an irrational desire to control an escalating situation and find a shortcut at all costs. I found that my frustration and impatience was dictating my walking, and that it brought me to these impasses. This approach of making impulsive decisions was putting me in danger. I had to let go of my pride and eat humble pie, admitting I was lost and turning around. The most difficult part was letting go of control,[35] accepting that the Camino was bigger than I was, and that I needed help and guidance to keep on track. Ironically, this had been Donal's downfall, being led by negative emotions and not taking advice. The experience was my introduction to a great insight: *you don't walk the Camino, it walks you.*

Eventually I retraced my steps to the village nearby. A local directed me back down the hill to Bolivar village, where, frustratingly, I had just come from. At this stage I could actually see the monastery where I was headed but would have to take a winding detour to get there. Those costly extra kilometers gave me time for reflection on detours, detachment, and what might have happened in terms of injury or getting lost. Fortunately, I was back on track shortly, this time with a new attitude and a respect for the arrows and guidebook.

In the afternoon I fell into step with my Dutch friend Adrian, whom I hadn't walked with for two days. Amazingly, I discovered he was seventy-five years old and fit as a fiddle. Not having any common language, we walked in silence, which suited us both. As we started up a huge hill covered in pine trees, I began to flag, but Adrian showed no signs of slowing down. I was glad of the company though, even as I trailed in his wake. We approached a farmyard and, out of habit, I picked up a stick from a hedge. A nasty-looking black dog tied up on a chain in a corner of the yard started snarling at us and suddenly came loose, making a beeline for us with feral ferocity. Adrian ducked behind me, and I beat the stick on the ground, holding the dog off with the point of it. In a bizarre waltz, we worked our way through the farmyard and retreated from the dog, which was now in a frenzy. The owner appeared, and I shouted angrily that his dog was free. Unfazed by the attack on us, he nonchalantly tied up the dog again to our great relief. It was another narrow escape in what was a stressful day. Some hours later, on the outskirts of Gernika, my energy was flagging and I ran out of water. I had to ask a local woman for assistance. Finding the albergue was easy, and after a quick meal, I had an early night.

The next morning was a slow start. Though it was still early as I walked the largely deserted streets out of Gernika, which had been nearly destroyed during the Spanish Civil War, a few bakeries and coffee shops were springing to life. There was no sign that this town had been bombed by the Germans seventy-four years earlier. I noticed some young people unsteady on their feet, obviously on their way home from the night before. I asked one young man for directions, and, reeking of liquor, he insisted on guiding me. He asked me where I was from, and upon hearing Northern Ireland, he went off on a tirade about the IRA and the "struggle for independence." The young man went on to tell me about the Basque fight for independence and how disappointed he was at the lack of results. He impressed on me the urgency of the struggle as he guided me onward, growing more animated and drawing me into a close camaraderie. I couldn't resist calling out, "*Vive la república!*" as we parted. My last memory was of him punching his fist in the air.

I began a steep ascent almost immediately, and I was back up in the mountains again shortly, alone on a high ridge. The rising sun slowly evaporated the mist lingering in the contours of the valleys. I was witnessing something transient but precious, the normally unseen transition to day. It touched me deeply, and tears welled up as I walked this pathway swathed in such beauty. Solitude here did not mean loneliness. Eventually I stopped for a rest at one of the many local houses that offered pilgrims water. I was heartened to see the group of Italians I had met a few days ago, who were now my friends. Twelve or so of us walkers spread out over the etapa during the day and would meet again at night. I stopped in a sleepy little village for the ubiquitous café con leche. The last part of the afternoon was tough, as unusually the Camino followed a main road, a sign we were getting close to Bilbao, the first big industrial city in the Basque Country. It made for fast walking, but it wasn't very pleasant—there was no scenic view, and the roar of cars dispelled any contemplative urge.

As I came to the town of Lezama, a well-dressed woman strode up the street for what I guessed was a church service. I followed her for about a kilometer until we came upon Iglesia de Santa María, a reddish stone church with an extensive veranda. I met some friendly people on the way who were interested in knowing who I was and

> **Ask for Grace**
> In prayer, it can be helpful to voice our true wants and desires, to ask God for the gift of these graces. When we do this, we align our desire with God's desire for us. Our prayer becomes concrete, and we become open to receiving God's gift.

where I had come from. The Catholic Mass was in Basque, which made it impossible to understand, but there was an unmistakable sense of community. My eyes focused on the striking baroque altarpiece in front of me. The red sandstone walls gave the nave a subtle glow that warmed my heart. Praying alone afterward, I felt some solace and asked for help with this walk as it seemed to be getting more difficult and beyond my abilities.[36]

As if in answer to my prayer, a woman came up and introduced herself. She was the local albergue coordinator (hospitalera) and invited me to accompany her to the hostel. I took it as a sign that my day's walking was over and felt relieved at her kindness. She embodied hospitality in her enthusiasm and knowledge and filled me in on the local services for pilgrims. She brought me to the hostel, and I showered and changed—a small, rejuvenating luxury. As she had to leave for a while, she asked me to look after the hostel. I was in my element in my newfound authority, checking people in and telling them where to place their bags. That evening at our pilgrim meal I realized we were becoming a small community: the Italians; my friend Adrian; Anuk, a Dutch woman between jobs; a Belgian dad getting away from it all; and a Spanish translator. We were bound by our common journey, our unique stories, and our flesh-and-blood humanity that was revealed by the road. Treasuring this moment and yet conscious of the constant challenges, I realized the levels of providence and exposure on the Camino demanded great flexibility: one had to be open to receiving great grace and providence, while at the same time, acknowledging this was often tied to hardship and vulnerability.

The next morning I couldn't believe my luck when I spotted a walking pole left behind in the recycling bin. Though there was only a single ski pole, it cheered me up enormously. I also picked up an old pair of hiking socks; I had been having trouble with my right foot and was convinced that these thicker socks would sort that out. Re-equipped and restored, I walked out of Lezama feeling great. Bilbao was ten kilometers away, and only a small hill lay in my path. On the ascent my left leg started to act up—a niggling pain at first and then a throbbing ache that I couldn't walk off. It was aggravated by the uphill climb, and I had no choice but to turn back.

The toughest part was passing my companions going the opposite way and having to wish them *Buen Camino*.[37] Hobbling off the hill and having to seek medical help was a bitter pill to swallow. Fortunately I was only one kilometer from the town of Zamudio, which was on the local rail network for Bilbao. While waiting, I noticed a pharmacy just outside the station. The chemist went to great lengths to help me with my sore leg, getting the right creams and tablets, though he advised me to check it out with a doctor. He also insisted I take some blister pads and foot cream at no charge. Glumly riding the train into town, I strained to see my friends on the brown hills. I wondered if they were okay, and especially if they were hydrated as the sun was fierce.

At this stage my foot was really hurting, and I didn't think I could walk much further. I limped my way to a suburb called Portugalete, which I thought would have plenty of services. I found the tourist office to ask for a *pensión* (cheap hotel) and directions for medical help. To my great relief, the man in the tourist office was exceptionally helpful. He gave me all the maps and addresses of the pensiónes and even located the local hospital for me. As it was late I would have to go the next day, so I basked outside in the sun by the river with a chorizo, cheese, and salad baguette. I was grateful for the man in the tourist office and all the good people I had met on this walk. Afterward I checked into a slightly seedy pensión overlooking the Nervión River. The shower didn't work, but I figured that you can't have everything. The staff, fortunately, were exceedingly friendly.

The next morning, I tried not to think about my companions trekking ahead of me on the next etapa. I could barely walk, and I dreaded finding out what was wrong. After breakfast I limped[38] up the hill to the hospital, anxious for some expert advice to resolve the issue. On a particularly steep street of Portugalete I asked directions from a woman selling lottery tickets. She casually suggested a health center directly behind her instead, saying it would save me time and effort. Intrigued, I went in and had to wait a few minutes to get processed. After fifteen minutes, I was seen by a friendly and efficient doctor. She had me diagnosed and dispatched in ten minutes, but it was not good news. She explained that the problem was *estrés tibial anterior,* an inflammation of the muscle causing pain in the shin bone (tibia), basically a shin splint. I could be out for a few weeks with this, in which case it would be game over. Or I could try resting it, rubbing in a special cream, and

> **Did you know . . .**
> St. Ignatius also walked with a limp. After a cannonball crushed his legs, he was bedridden for eight months. He had his leg rebroken twice to fix a protruding bone, and a cannonball was hung from one leg to stretch it out. Though these were vain attempts to fix his limp, the painful process helped lead him to conversion.

taking anti-inflammatories for the pain. I would know the outcome in a few days.

With mixed emotions I walked gingerly down the hill to my friendly pensión. The owner was sympathetic and inquired after my diagnosis and treatment. The ignominy of having to return home early tore into my consciousness. How would I face family and friends who had sponsored me? Faced with the prospect of sitting around aimlessly for several days, I knew I had to get away. I called my friend José de Pablo, a Jesuit who lived in Burgos, some 120 kilometers away. It would be a break from the Camino, but I could still return and resume where I left off. José kindly dropped everything and drove to Bilbao to pick me up.

Packing in the fading luxury of the pensión, I was in a low mood, thinking this might be the end of my Camino. My injury put the whole experience into sharp focus, now that it might be ending. There was something powerfully compelling, almost addictive, about walking the Camino. It was tough, physically and mentally, and there were few luxuries, but it was profoundly rewarding. The payoff was the elusive "being in the moment" awareness and the falling away of other concerns. There was a real connection on the trail—with others, oneself, and the world. And there was something real and embodied about Camino life, as close and personal as breathing, but at the same time transcendent and sacred. Simple memories, such as tying my shoes, swinging my rucksack on my back, and breathing deeply when faced with the Iberian unknown, had been utterly thrilling.

The Camino always challenged me: What would happen that day? Whom would I meet? Would I find openness in myself and others? Would I find life and consolation? For Ignatius it was about being sensitive to the divine, speaking in and through the ordinary events of the day.[39] For me, it was often only after the event, reflecting back on it, that I could clearly see God working to take care of me, challenging me and leading me in very concrete ways. Being a pilgrim strips away protective insulation and accentuates the sense of trusting dependency, stepping out into the unknown. Every day is an act of trust, believing that all will be resolved on the road. However, this reminiscing was making me forlorn, wishing I were back on the road where my heart was. On the other hand, a tiny voice reminded me about the fatigue, the uncertainty, the hostels, the snoring at night, the lack of comfort, the exposure in all weathers—things I wouldn't miss.

I left my backpack at reception and went out to wait for José. I wondered if I would be back this way again and whether I would ever hoist my pack for another day's walking on the Camino. My only hope was that, like Ignatius, this injury would mean something greater, a bigger plan over which I had no control.[40]

# 4

# Solitary Confinement

The E804 highway proved very noisy and very fast. Driving an old battered Renault, my Jesuit friend José ran a deluge of questions in Spanish past me. It was lovely to see him, but I struggled to adjust to this radically different environment of overpasses, traffic lanes, and speeding cars. There was not one hiker to be seen. Ironically, after all the sweat and toil I had put into the twelve days of walking to Bilbao, the same distance would now be covered in little over an hour. It somehow felt like cheating and was disorientating; all my normal referents of albergues, yellow arrows (*flechas amarillas*), trails (*caminos*), and pilgrims (*peregrinos*) were absent. I missed my walking companions, and I felt like I was betraying them, going off like this. The thought that this fast escape might be my only good-bye to them brought a lump to my throat.

All I could do was engage with my new situation as wholeheartedly as I could. I had made the best decision I could in Bilbao—to heal and rest—and rehashing it would be unhelpful and disruptive.[41] I turned to

> One of Ignatius's useful guidelines for decision making is to never go back on a decision you made when you were in consolation, grounded, or in a time of balance. Being too high or too low are also poor times to decide.

look at José more clearly. What a blessing it was to be rescued by a familiar face in another country.

I had a great fondness for José, whom I had not seen for six years since we studied and worked together in Dublin. We had been students in the same theology program and had lived close to each other south of the river Liffey. I had brought him on many sightseeing trips in Ireland, and now the situation was reversed. We had lots

> Spiritual direction offers a companion for our spiritual journey, a guide who can more easily spot our movements and unfreedoms. Spiritual directors actively listen, helping us find freedom, make balanced decisions, and grow closer to God.

of stories to tell to bring each other up to date (*ponernos al día*). It turned out we were both engaged in youth work, and we quickly realized we could collaborate on some common projects. José remained silent as I told him the story of our family's loss and the reason for this Camino walk. He understood, and I felt heard.[42]

As we drove alongside the river Arlanzón, Burgos looked dry, hot, and built up. It was a far cry from a mountain path in the Basque region. I really felt like I was back in civilization when I was shown to a single room with a bed and a sink. These were rare luxuries. There wasn't a bunk bed or a communal shower in sight. It felt strange to have blinds on the windows and to be living in the half-light of the indoors. I jumped at the offer to wash all my greying clothes in a machine, my hand washing not having been up to scratch. I was given a tour of the Jesuit school, and it felt odd to be introduced by my title (*Padre Jesuita, capellán*—Jesuit priest, chaplain) and not just by my first name, as on the Camino.

That night José invited me out for an ice cream with another Jesuit, an artist named Jaime.[43] Sitting in the main plaza, I recounted my Camino adventure and how it had been cut short by injury. Walking by the river on the way home, Jaime took me aside and explained that he, too, had walked the Camino. "Your injury," he said, "is actually part of the Camino—maybe the most important part." Intrigued, I pressed him to say more. "It's a process," he said, "much more than a simple walk, and it's what happens interiorly [in your mental and spiritual being] that matters. It is not about simply walking the trail; many people do this and often learn nothing. If you can embrace this seemingly negative experience of injury, you will get closer to the heart of the Camino."

I really wanted to agree with him, but it seemed too much to hope that this setback could actually be something positive for me. (I had heard anecdotally that many pilgrims give up at this point.) Then he added, "The Camino is actually more powerful than doing the Spiritual Exercises retreat of St. Ignatius."[44] Now this was something I hadn't heard before, but it was exciting as he gave the Spiritual Exercises a new framework, one that was perfectly in line with Ignatian spirituality. Ignatius always defined himself as "the pilgrim" and would have walked the Camino trails.

I asked, "What was it about your Camino experience that made it the ultimate retreat?" But he merely tapped his finger on the side of his nose. I would have to wait and see whether his insight was true. If it was, I was really only beginning. However, at that moment, my injury was the greatest test, infinitely more frustrating than actually walking the trail. Still, there was room for some deeper learning here, and it gave me new hope for my own journey.

The next day I discovered a bedazzling architectural jewel. Turning a corner, I came upon the soaring thirteenth-century Gothic cathedral Santa María de Burgos. The flying buttresses, delicate arches, and towers all made it seem like it was shimmering in the warm air. Its white ashlar masonry launched it skyward, in sharp contrast with its surroundings. In the nave I was mesmerized by the transcendent effect of the light, a reddish pink radiance. The impossibly fine pillars drew my eyes up to discover the source of this light. Indeed, I had heard that Gothic architecture's purpose was to elevate the mind and spirit to the contemplation of heavenly things. I could imagine Ignatius of Loyola gazing up at these soaring pillars, head flung back,[45] although there is no evidence of his ever being here.

Coming back to earth from my heavenly trip, I came across a familiar-looking scallop shell set into the pavement outside the cathedral. I had intended to get away from the Camino for a while, but, of course, here I was right on the principal route, the Camino Francés. This French route runs right past the cathedral, and within a few minutes I spotted a steady stream of pilgrims passing in different states of repair. I recognized the perspiring faces, the bulging backpacks, the grimaces, and the giveaway limps. The intense heat, around eighty-six degrees, made for much tougher walking and confirmed my choice of the coastal route. And yet I was still seized by a mad urge to introduce myself as a fellow pilgrim, even though I wasn't a pilgrim and had no gear. I identified with their endeavor and the significance of their slog. I wanted it so badly, I even briefly thought about continuing the French route from here. But I was still officially out of action.

The next day I woke with a sense of D-day: it was time to decide whether I was going back on the Camino. I had to know if my leg had healed. I decided to wear the backpack and practice on the stairs in the Jesuit residence. If I felt pain at all, I promised myself, I would call it quits. To my great relief, even though there was soreness and sensitivity around the muscle next to the shin, I felt no real pain. Even then, I knew that going ahead would be a calculated risk—there were so many things that could go wrong.

*What would Ignatius do?* I thought. He probably would have asked if I had taken the usual measures, such as seeking medical help and getting rest, which I had. He would have been concerned about inflicting permanent injury on myself, which seemed unlikely here.

Finally, he would have asked if my burning desire to return to the Camino was misguided, and to look more dispassionately at the issues.[46] These included managing my injury well, going gently, planning support along the way should it happen again, and trying to be free of the pressure from my sponsors and supporters. I took some time over the decision; there was a lot riding on it. At last clarity and peace came, and my heart fairly soared as I decided I would continue. This was not to be the end of the story.

Later that day, I took a bus from Burgos back to Bilbao and said *adios*[47] to my dear friend José. He had been so kind and helpful to me during a low point. As I was getting out of the car, he promised he would arrange for me to stay in other Jesuit houses on the route if I needed. On the bus out of Burgos I felt a mix of emotions: sadness, but also excitement and nervousness. On the edge of the city we crossed the Camino Francés, and I could see it was fairly thronged with walkers in the afternoon heat. The route was rough and primitive but with a unique charm in its solitude. As the Basque Country crept into view, I was struck by how mountainous and green and temperate it was. I felt ready to face the Camino del Norte again. I hoped the Way would treat me well.

As soon as I stepped off the bus in Bilbao, a giant sign, *Rebajas* [Sale] *50%*, in the window of a hiking shop drew my attention. I was drawn inside before I knew it. There were endless rows of shorts, shell layers, and fleeces, not to mention ropes, boots, and crampons. And there were brand-new shiny hiking poles. . . . I wasn't even back on the Camino, and yet here I was in hiker heaven, surrounded by the best gear at a huge discount. Exhilarated, I raced around the aisles, checking prices and brands, and unintentionally knocked over some stands with my backpack. As the salesperson bore down on me, I knew that my freedom would be short-lived.

Then the most curious feeling came over me, like I was detached from my surroundings. A creeping calm seemed to whisper, "You don't actually need any of this stuff," and "This purchase will not bring you any real pleasure or help your Camino." A wave of relief washed over me, and the manic-like tension that had held me drained away. I happen to have a thing for hiking shops, and I felt overrun by this desire. But here, seen through the Camino lens, this materialist impulse was clearly at odds with the simple hiker lifestyle.

Viscerally, I felt something clarify within me, like putting on new glasses. The fierce grip of possessing, of being attached to things, was released. Even from a practical point of view, I had carefully packed for the absolute minimum, and I couldn't afford extras. So apart from possibly replacing the poles, which weren't essential, I already had everything I needed. Ignatius, the ultimate pilgrim, would have understood this completely: to be free of those things that hinder progress, especially unhelpful attachments.[48]

> The modern interpretation of freedom is often "freedom from" commitments and worries. Ignatius would have understood freedom as "freedom for" living life fully and "freedom from" unhealthy attachments, such as compulsions or addictions.

My brother Donal had also been a great model for how to be free from possessions. He cared not for appearance or for wealth; he would give away money, clothes, his car, his time, as casually as breathing. You merely had to say you liked a jacket of his, and it was yours, or that you needed a lift, and he had his keys in hand. He had this beat-up Toyota that he would leave unlocked, sometimes with the keys in it, inviting anyone to steal it. Traveling abroad with him was challenging because he would throw a few things in a bag and arrive at the airport at the last second. Nothing was planned or prepared for; he just trusted that he would be looked after. He owned some apartments and made a point of having the most unlikely tenants, especially people in difficult circumstances. Often, this chaotic approach would cause him all sorts of problems, but it all came from Donal's deep desire to help others, to be free of material things, and to live from the heart. I felt particularly close to him as I shouldered my pack.

I made my way out to the lovely fishing port of Castro-Urdiales on the outskirts of Bilbao. The harbor was breathtaking with its boats and historic buildings. While waiting for the hostel to open, I toured a lovely twelfth-century Gothic church, Santa María, and then visited the dramatic castle and lighthouse on the point. Walking the deserted boardwalk, I toyed with the idea of a swim. Suddenly, a huge Saint Bernard bounded up, jumping up on me playfully. Almost immediately a young woman appeared with a boxer, and the two dogs ferociously attacked each other. Terrified, the woman started screaming, "Pull him off, get your dog away!" assuming I was the owner. Shocked at the speed of events, I was reluctant to get involved in this whirl of teeth and snapping jaws. Eventually, I managed to get the Saint Bernard away by shouting and making cattle-herding moves. As the Saint Bernard took off over the rise, the young woman also disappeared. It was all over—except for my accelerated heartbeat. What just happened? Was this a test of my own freedom, my willingness to respond and get involved? I wasn't sure, but the graphic image of canine violence was burned in my consciousness. I walked around cautiously the rest of the afternoon. Even with the rucksack my leg felt fine, though tender. I intended to take the next stage at a much gentler pace.

The hostel was hard to find, way out on the edge of town. The evening sky was illuminated with bonfires and fireworks marking the summer solstice and the feast of San Juan. Inside the *refugio* (refuge, basic hostel), I felt like a Camino rookie, so slow in organizing my bunk and gear. I had hoped to meet my friends from before but was disappointed not to recognize anyone. My companions now were mainly taciturn Germans and Austrians. I found it hard to let go; I was stuck in expectations about what kind of experience I wanted—another thing to let go of. Like good pilgrims, we were all in bed by ten for that crucial early start.

The following morning found me on the road at six-thirty, slipping easily into the old routine. On the elevated coastal path the first light was sublime: the sun rose directly out of the sea and was diffused through a ribbon of clouds. My heart burned[49] with gratitude and anticipation.

*There is nowhere else I'd rather be in the world right now*, I thought. Even though my left leg was still sore and I walked gingerly, I prayed with emotion: *This is enough for me.*[50] No one else was around to witness this historic moment: my second attempt at the Camino.

> This prayer is a modern translation of St. Ignatius's Suscipe:
>
> *Take, Lord, and receive all my liberty,*
> *my memory, my understanding,*
> *and my entire will,*
> *All I have and call my own.*
> *You have given all to me.*
> *To you, Lord, I return it.*
>
> *Everything is yours; do with it what you will.*
> *Give me only your love and your grace,*
> *that is enough for me.*
>
> —St. Ignatius of Loyola, SE 234

Fortunately, the route was fairly flat and well-paved as I meandered along the Cantabrian coast. At one stage I walked through a herd of goats, the brilliant sea to my right and a huge mountain to the left. *I will remember this moment forever*, I thought. I was so happy—happy to be alive and taking in this magical coast, but also grateful I wasn't on a plane returning home. Each step became a treasured gift. I realized again the precariousness of this quest, that I might not finish the Camino at all or even get to the next village. Paradoxically, this thought freed me, made me appreciate every little advance and moment. Knowing I couldn't control the Camino helped me surrender to it more fully.

Turning inland, I arrived in Rioseco (Dry River) before noon and had a coffee at a bar with my own crudely made sandwiches. I had walked thirteen kilometers without any problems, and although most of it was flat, it felt like a great achievement. The afternoon walk on the map showed an uphill route, and not wanting to push my leg too hard, I decided to bypass the mountain and take a twenty-minute bus ride instead. The woman behind the bar was extremely helpful, but I was disappointed to learn that the next bus would not leave for another four hours. Looking at the map, I thought I found an alternative route. I set off in the wrong direction, however, which a man in a wheelchair informed me of two kilometers later. There was nothing I could do but return to the bar and wait for the bus. At least the bar had shade to prevent me from melting in the afternoon heat. I also had time to reflect on the day, which was great initially and then went off track later. I really was a slow learner. However, I had a strong sense that all these detours and injuries were teaching me. Mostly I just needed to slow down and be more patient, accepting the gift inherent in a situation without looking to better it.

It was early evening when I arrived in Laredo, very late for the hostels. As rooms were in short supply, four other German pilgrims from the bus and I made a beeline for the tourist office. I found a hostel nearby, *El Buen Pastor*, run by the Good Shepherd sisters. With both single and double rooms, the hostel was a notch above any other and accordingly more expensive. After trekking up and down corridors with a flustered nun, we learned that all the rooms were taken. Explaining that I was a Jesuit priest helped thaw out the stress I had caused her and seemed to give her an idea. So after a delay, she came back to tell me she had organized a room for me with the Trinitarian nuns, an enclosed order in the Convento de San Francisco nearby.

Tired by now, I walked slowly over to the imposing convent door and rang the bell. As if by magic the door sprung open. I climbed the silent monastery stairs with some anticipation and was met by a ruddy-faced nun in full habit. Wordlessly she brought me to an isolated room in a corner of the monastery. She stamped my credencial, I paid her the room fee of €10, and off she glided into the cloister. The silence, far from awkward, was liberating. The Camino had taught me the value of that. I studied my unique stamp, *Monjas Trinitarias-Laredo*, with delight. Quite a boon, this room turned out to be much better lodgings than I could have imagined. Though there were no windows and the bathroom was so small I couldn't do laundry, I appreciated what I had. I ignored all the dead mosquitoes on the walls, which wouldn't help me sleep peacefully. After reflecting on a good day, I slept very well. Like a monk in a silent monastery, I enjoyed my solitary confinement.

# 5
# Too Much of a Good Thing

Back in the seaside town of Laredo, the deadly drone of a mosquito forced me out of bed. I guessed that it had already bitten me, which would manifest into an irritating itch later. I knew now why the room was plastered with dead mosquitoes. Food was not included in this unique monastery deal, so after packing, I headed straight to the expansive surf beach. Lined with hotels and apartments, the beach was deserted at this early hour, and I had the sandy wilderness all to myself. At the end of the shore was a ferry across to another town, Santoña, which would save me a lot of walking. Ahead of me stretched a vast sand flat, a great crescent that swept around into a rocky headland, resplendent in a perfect sunrise.

Leaning into the stiff breeze, I hugged myself with glee, savoring this breathless moment. Hungry for breakfast, I scanned the ragged line of bars and hotels. A lone walker told me nothing was open and to follow the beach around the point for the ferry. This took me well over an hour, particularly as there was no sign for where the ferry pulled in. As I was early, I sat on a sandy shelf and was delighted to discover some fruit and chocolate in my backpack.

The ferry, more like a glorified launch, plowed straight into the shore to make a gangway for the ten or so people waiting. Hearing the accents, I picked out two young Irish women, Carol and Fiona, who were teachers on their first Camino experience. We swapped stories over coffee on Santoña's promenade. Kitted out in brand-new gear, they were taking a week on the northern route and then going south for a beach holiday. It quickly transpired that they were rookies on the Camino and were finding it tough, especially as their priority was to have a holiday. I found myself in the unlikely role of the "seasoned veteran," having been on the Camino for longer. I sympathized with them and gladly gave them all my hard-earned tips.

However, I knew it wouldn't be long before they called it a day. Afterward I thought about what a crucial role motivation plays and how the Camino really tests people. It is a fire that purifies commitment, determining how much people want to do it. For these women it determined how the walk was experienced—that is,

> Ignatian freedom is about accepting situations as gifts without being limited by preconceptions or expectations. When we aren't weighed down by what *could* have been or what *should* be, we are free to meet God and his gifts of grace right where we are.

punishing as opposed to enjoyable. The same experience of hostels, basic facilities, strenuous exercise, and mediocre food can be interpreted in vastly different ways.[51]

The typical Camino image is one of trails and hills, but from Laredo on, it was mostly beach walking. Walking along a pristine sandy beach by a whispering ocean, I almost felt guilty for relishing the experience. After having had my fill of mud, forest, and mountain, here was dramatic coastal scenery more befitting to vacationers. Almost immediately I came on the unspoiled beach of Berria, which was empty except for a few walkers, surfers, and fishermen. The Camino route ran parallel with the beach, and it seemed infinitely preferable to walk on the sand, enjoying the beach vistas and windblown casualness. I was sorry to come onto a headland where I had to climb cautiously while protecting my leg.

But this was not the end—the view further down the coast revealed a string of indented sandy shores. Directly in front of me was the thronged, touristy beach of Helgueras. Even though it was scarred with rocky veins, Helgueras was another sandy haven, open to the turquoise sea and sky. People were everywhere, swimming, picnicking, walking, and playing games. It was a strange contrast between the holiday makers in swimwear and the line of hikers with backpacks, poles, and sun hats cutting a swath through them. They strode with military intensity and purpose in mountain boots, paying little attention to the relaxation and fun around them. I stopped for lunch at a rocky outcrop and threw off my gear to temporarily enjoy some beach atmosphere.

Just when it seemed that this seaside delight would never end, the Camino took a turn inland at Trengandín beach near the town of Noja. I was fortunate to fall in with a group of Dutch people and a lone Spanish woman, as I was lost. Incredibly, there were no more yellow arrows on the road, and my guidebook was vague and useless. In a roadside huddle we realized we were all lost. I was relieved when a young Dutch woman took the lead and confidently directed us for many kilometers through a maze of roads and paths. At one point we had to cross a salt marsh and passed some stone water mills on a tidal estuary—an act of trust as there were no signs or landmarks. On and on we went through nondescript lanes, valleys, and fields. At one point a huge eagle pounced on some prey right beside me, an eerie reminder not to get separated from the group.

The Spanish woman started to lag behind, and the Dutch woman, with admirable patience, had us all wait for her. The Spanish woman strolled along nonchalantly, unbalanced by her backpack on one shoulder, talking loudly on the phone and smoking a cigarette. It seemed the epitome of relaxed style, but something didn't quite fit. Upon reaching us, she lost her temper, asking whose idea this route was and complaining that she should have known better, that she always preferred to go on her own. Patiently, the Dutch woman showed her where we were on the map and assured her we were not lost. It was a model of how to deal with a difficult person using compassion and kindness. I doubted I would have been able to see the positive side and react to her so well.[52]

We stopped at a hillside bar for some ice cream, where the Spanish woman again took an inordinate amount of time. The Dutch woman made sure she knew where we were going and what the route was, and then we left her there. Everyone breathed a collective sigh of relief, and we began making more progress. Little did I realize I would be meeting her again soon.

We were in rolling Cantabrian farming country, patchwork crops and forest, but the throbbing in my feet made it hard to think about anything else. We walked through a pass in the mountains and then into another valley where the familiar yellow arrows again pointed the way. At my limit, I was so glad to see the signs for the hostel and appreciative of the Dutch group for their company and guidance.

When we arrived in Güemes some grueling hours later, we could be forgiven for thinking we had arrived in paradise. There were people to greet us, water and fruit to eat as we sat down, and exceptional hospitality from volunteers[53] who, as former pilgrims, knew what it was like to arrive footsore and hungry. The rural, hilltop hostel, *La Cabaña del Abuelo Peuto*, was custom-made for hikers, with lots of bright, airy rooms. After I signed in, an eager volunteer gave me a tour and showed me to my spacious bunkroom. Afterward I was invited to a communal dinner made by the volunteer hospitaleros. Incredibly, they asked only for a voluntary donation to cover all. It was a radical departure from the minimalistic albergues in which I had previously stayed.

That night the head hospitalero called all the walkers together for what was a first for me: a briefing on the next day's walk. I was volunteered as the English translator. The hospitalero mapped out the next etapa, which would finish in the great city of Santander, but we had a choice of routes: a direct road route or a longer coastal path. Afterward, someone took out a guitar and some wine, and we had a great sing-along, which I couldn't resist joining. This was what I had missed in other hostels—a strong sense of community, fun, and sharing. As I lay in my bunk, content with the full day, I made a note in my blog: "Possibly the best hostel I've stayed in: a rare combination of eating together, talking, and sharing experiences." Someone had told me this community experience was much more typical of the Camino Francés hostels.

I woke to a cold and crisp morning, perfect walking weather. I made a point of saying good-bye to the volunteers and the distinctive albergue in Güemes. As I marched down the country road, I fell into step with Willy, a German man I had met the previous night. He was tall and thin, wearing round horn-rimmed glasses and no hat, which made him squint in the strong sunlight. We had no common language, but he had an amazing knack for communicating with whistles and gestures that was endearing. Eventually we came to a major road and the choice of routes we had been told about. Even though it was considerably longer, the advantages of the coastal route readily convinced us.

Shortly we came to some sheer cliffs with a trail right along the edge. The view of isolated beaches, blue-green ocean, and clear sky was intoxicating. The morning mist clung to the contours of the receding cliffs, reinforcing the silence that held us spellbound. The pristine Cantabrian coastline spoke of the beauty of creation. Looking back, we saw a line of some twenty pilgrims on the same route. Eventually they caught up with us, and rather than race ahead, we let them go, finding a dramatic clifftop aerie where we could contemplate the vast seascape below.

Eventually we rejoined the trail and met a number of young Germans, one of whom seemed to be leading the way. I recognized him from the briefing the night before where he had also helped with the translation. We came again to a decision point where the Camino headed inland, but there was a rough path along the rocky shore. Instinctively I plunged ahead on the coast but was soon halted by a rocky headland that was difficult to scale with backpacks. The young German man remonstrated me for disobeying the guidebook and taking a wrong turn. I was beyond caring about the book at this stage; I could smell the sea and wanted to be close to it.

Eventually we came to a famous surf beach, Arenal del Puntal, and were back among dozens of holiday makers. The hard, wet sand was a pleasure to hike along, and the noise of the breakers hypnotic. Willy and I stopped for a snack in the shade of some boulders; he had a stove for brewing tea, a rare luxury. Forty minutes later we arrived in the town of Somo, and, running late, we sprinted across a sandy spit to the ferry for Santander. Being on the boat was a treat, to rest our legs and be swept across the sea. It was exhilarating to sweep into the huge port of Santander and imagine what it would have been like for pilgrims arriving centuries ago.

After our group of hikers went to the tourist office to get maps and find the hostels, we sought out the Gothic Catedral de Nuestra Señora de la Asunción. Our timing was perfect as inside the sun streamed through the columns in the old cloister. The interplay of light and stone in honeyed hues was as inspiring as I imagine it was for the original medieval monks too. The main cathedral was packed with clergy, dignitaries, and worshipers for the celebration of Corpus Christi. After celebrating Mass, an elaborate procession, which the Spanish excel at, marched around the city. Seeing the Blessed

Sacrament on the move, I had a curious feeling of walking with the pilgrim Christ, who was my guide on this journey, even though I often couldn't see too far ahead.

Midafternoon, the other hikers tried to persuade me to accompany them to the hostel. Stubbornly I refused, insisting I had to get out of the city and into the country to make up lost time. Alone again, I took a metro to the suburbs and got off where the city ran out. Immediately I met an Italian couple who had booked a hotel on the Camino and were fretfully trying to find it. I found myself getting caught up in their anxiety. Initially they helped me get back on track, but afterward I was left with a heavy heart. Should I have stayed with them, taking the easy option? Without any clear destination, I continued my solitary trudge uphill. I had an uneasy feeling that I had missed or misplaced something important.

I toiled up an endless hill in oppressive afternoon heat, eventually coming to the hilltop village of Mogro, which was little more than a church and a square. My guidebook stated that the parish priest of the local church, San Martín, was very welcoming to pilgrims and that there was some makeshift accommodation at the church. However, when I asked next door, they told me the priest had moved and that he only came on Sundays for Mass. They did offer to open the church porch for me though and let me take a siesta there to get through the worst of the heat. The flagstones were delicious—a cool remedy for the feet—and the concrete bench felt like a feather bed. After an hour's rest, I reluctantly set off again in the intense heat, getting more and more ill-tempered as sweat obscured my vision and blisters began to boil up on my feet.

I was now committed to walking across an arid hill to Polanco, an industrial area where I knew there was a municipal hostel. This was exactly the situation I didn't want to be in: caught between hostels and having to walk on asphalt in the searing heat. I began to limp; blisters hurt my feet, and I could find no relief from the eighty-six-degree heat. By now, far from the coast, all the inspiring seascapes were gone. Burnt grass and dust dominated. It turned into a grim marathon, and I regretted my decision to push on.

Even though I had thought continuing was the best option and had justified it to myself, I felt deceived.[54] The good I had sought turned out to be misleading or deceptive. I realized how important Ignatius's notion of "balance"[55] was, how a seemingly good desire can become distorted and lead me in the wrong direction. An image formed in my head of a scale or a spinning top being tipped out of balance by excess weight or pressure. Ignatius knew about this imbalance through bitter experience, suffering the ravages of his own extreme behavior, attachments, and destructive impulses.[56]

> Like standing in the center of a seesaw, St. Ignatius urges us to cultivate balance—to be poised at equilibrium, without tipping too much to either side and getting compromised. When we're balanced, we're open and ready to follow God wherever he calls us.

I had seen this same dynamic in Donal. His passion and great love of life sometimes got turned against him. There seemed to be some malign spirit undermining his talent for helping others, making friends, and enjoying himself. Being totally available and trying to please others often caused him great sadness and depression. He was too good for his own good, as we said at his funeral. I could see something similar working in me now: being seduced by something that seemed good (walking further), but was actually damaging.[57]

How had I been led so far off track, so far off balance? I realized I had exceeded my body's limits again, overriding my earlier "take it easy" wisdom. I had wrongly prioritized getting out of the city over rest and recovery. Simply accepting the mild inconvenience of a city hostel would have saved me a lot of pain.

Ignatius had this great rule of thumb[58] about decisions: even though something seems obvious and straightforward and may have worked before, you have to examine it carefully and pray about it to ensure it's genuinely good. Something clearly negative is easy to spot, but that which appears good on the surface, a subtle form of deception, can be misleading. Ignatius called this the deception of the "Angel of Light,"[59] or how we get derailed by *apparent* goods. He designed a canny method for thoroughly examining "attractive" ideas to uncover hidden traps, something I would remember.[60] I had lost my balance,[61] to use Ignatius's metaphor, and I had learned a valuable lesson, but it would just be a temporary setback if I could recover my poise and get back on track. Wearily, I resolved to make the most of it.

> St. Ignatius's Rules for Discernment provide us with tried-and-true guidelines for making decisions. These methods and tips highlight common pitfalls, help us monitor our moods, reveal our motivations in being driven or drawn to make a decision, and, ultimately, show us our true desires and help us move forward.

Further down the road one man stopped his car to give me directions, and I craved the air-conditioned coolness within. A number of other people were also helpful on the road, but I was grimly hanging on. I hobbled into Polanco, a distinctly industrial town, in the late afternoon and found the Quin (short for "Joaquin") Bar. A kind, elderly woman, Señora Ascensión, gave me the keys and indicated the albergue a further five hundred meters down the road in a small depression. I thought she was mistaken at first—it looked like an electricity substation or a low barn. She showed me into what was possibly the unlikeliest hostel in the world, with only two narrow rooms and three bunks in each. An Italian couple had taken one room, so I had the other to myself.

It was an enormous relief to get inside and away from the heat. Bathed in sweat with throbbing feet, I collapsed into a chair and had a cold soft drink. Every tangy drop tasted like heaven. I had a go at puncturing my blisters but ended up making a mess of them. Entering the shower, the floor was swimming in water, soap scum and human hair. All I could do was delicately tiptoe over and get under the cold water quickly. Coming back to my bunk, I noticed that the covers on the beds, once cream, were now smoky brown.

I dreaded going back up to the bar for food, but I had no choice; there was nowhere else to go in this factory zone. Señora brought me to an empty room off the bar and offered me a great deal: three courses for €9. Hunger negated all thoughts about it being hygienic. The salad was a bit tired and the spaghetti lame, but I ate and enjoyed it all. When we came back to the micro-hostel, the two Italians were asleep, and I was a dead man walking. Entombed in the oppressive heat, I was so tired I fell into a dreamless sleep.

# 6

# Walking on Broken Glass

Dawn came as an unwelcome guest in the shabby Polanco hostel. I tried keeping my eyes shut for as long as possible, putting off the moment when I would have to face reality again. The hostel didn't improve in daylight, and though I was trying to make the best of it, it was hard not to see the squalor in the dirty floors and bed covers. Arriving uninvited came the thought *worst hostel I have stayed in*, but I resisted breaking the Camino rule about being ungrateful for anything. This simple rule had served me well and left me free to accept whatever else, good or bad, was coming down the line.[62] This place had provided me with food and shelter at one of my worst moments; it was a timely refuge.[63] I briefly considered staying on in the albergue and getting medical help, but I knew that pilgrims could stay only one night per hostel. The Italian couple next door had gone without a sound, and I hadn't even spoken a word to them. I made an equally silent and rapid exit from this timely but grubby shelter,

> When we begin to notice all the gifts we've received from God—from the sun streaking through fall leaves to a call from a good friend—it's difficult not to respond with gratitude and want to return this love. Ignatius calls us to see everything as a gift and God as the giver, and to feel our hearts transformed in a grateful, loving response.

which had met my needs despite my grumblings. I said a little prayer of gratitude and touched the lintel as I left.[64]

As I hoisted the backpack and my feet hit the pavement, the pain began again. I had almost forgotten about the blisters, presuming that like most problems they would be cured by sleep and rest, but they were back with a vengeance, now with a jangly nerve pain from cracked and torn skin. The experience felt like walking on broken glass in bare feet. Feeling even more of a fool for having overdone it the day before, I was determined to walk through the pain and put it behind me. *Sometimes the start is the worst*, I told myself, and set about gritting my teeth and ignoring the discomfort. Seeking distraction, I looked to either side but saw only deserted rows of warehouses, electrical pylons, and car parks. I felt like I was lost in a featureless industrial zone, with few signs of human habitation or nature's transcendent beauty. The bleak environment echoed my inner world like some dreadful pathetic fallacy, where the emotions shape the surroundings.

When one foot became unbearably painful, I sought to favor the other. Limping along with the rucksack became progressively harder. Hungry, I was holding out for a café or bar to have breakfast and get relief from the pain to assess the situation. Normally I would have brought some food from the night before, but nothing had been available. It was exactly 7:00 a.m. when I came upon a bar full of builders and truckers. The décor was 1970s minimalism combined with macho functionalism. A backpack, shorts, and sun hat were suddenly incongruous. Grimacing on my way to the bar to order, I knew then I wouldn't be walking much further that day. The pain from the broken blisters was much more acute than the day before, and I dared not take off my socks to look at them. A lame hiker stranded between worlds, I found a remote window table with a view of van roofs and trucks. I spread out my map on the faded laminate table in the vain hope of examining what few options I had left.

Failing to work their normal magic, my coffee and a croissant brought no tangible relief. What weighed heaviest was the knowledge that I had to get away from this predominantly commercial area and get some urgent medical attention. I would have to step off the Camino again and leave all that went with it. Integrating that decision and acting upon it were still beyond me, however—I needed time to work through all the false voices and inner critics that wanted me to ignore the problem and keep going. I could hear a voice admonishing me for failing again, betraying my mission, and taking the easy way out. I had to sit tight and wait out the storm of emotion,

> How to act against desolation:
>
> 1. Tell God how you feel and ask for help.
> 2. Seek out companionship.
> 3. Don't go back on decisions you made in consolation.
> 4. Stand still and remember your inner map.
> 5. Recall a time of consolation, and go back to it in imagination.
> 6. Look for someone who needs your help, and turn your attention toward that person.
> 7. Go back to 1.
>
> —Excerpted from Margaret Silf's *Inner Compass*

differing desires, and conflicting motivations, the true desires revealing themselves with time.[65] Getting help, though humbling, was the right thing to do. Getting back on the Camino was up in the air.

As I sat at that table, I could see the Camino recede from me again, ruled out by my own rashness and misplaced zeal. Sometime later I came to the necessary decision to ask the barman for the nearest doctor, and he told me how to catch a bus there. I got directions to the bus stop, which was still a considerable walk involving a considerable amount of pain. But I was feeling much better now that I had a clear purpose.[66] I ignored my normal routine of applying sunscreen and putting on my hat. *I won't need those anymore*, I thought. At the main highway, I found the bus stop beside a dilapidated church. *Where is God in this experience of humiliating defeat?*[67] I wondered, fed up with this second major setback. I boarded the bus for the short journey to Santillana del Mar, where I would get medical attention. It was still only nine in the morning, and I was done for the day, maybe for the whole Camino.

I was so fed up I hardly noticed the medieval stone buildings, the historic center, and the many tourists in Santillana. I alighted beside the Santa Clara Convent, a terracotta and sandstone building. I briefly toyed with whether I would throw myself on their mercy, like a poor wounded medieval pilgrim, seeking sanctuary to heal and recover. Dismissing that idea, I set about finding the medical center, which was only meters from where the bus left me. Santillana's *consultorio médico* was in a low brownstone building. Fortified by my positive medical experience in Bilbao, I expectantly joined the queue. It quickly became apparent, however, that this would be a very different experience.

A stressed secretary struggled to cope with the swelling numbers. She was getting frustrated with her computer and with those in front of her. In turn, people were getting impatient, gesturing and protesting. I could see this coming down the line as I drew closer: the foreigner without proper documents who was going to cause an even bigger holdup. Sure enough, I was met by a wall of irritation and short-temperedness, implying that I was causing great annoyance. I asked Ignatius to give me strength for this particular ordeal.[68] It took all my reserves of patience and compassion, all the while with my feet on fire, to go through the extensive paperwork, fend off the emotional undertow, and not respond in kind. An hour later I got my appointment, as first I had to go to a nearby bank to pay a fee into their account before they'd see me.

Walking into the doctor's office was like entering a different world—one of tranquillity, peace, and order. The doctor was kind and efficient, and after a brief look passed me on to a nurse who injected the blisters with some kind of disinfectant. She put two white chunky pads over the balls of my feet, telling me to rest for at least one day. Walking out, I felt like I was floating on air as the pain had largely gone. Being treated was one thing, but having the problem solved and being offered the hope of continuing the Camino was invaluable. I treated myself to a cheap room in a boarding house (*posada*), marveling at the delights of a single room, and immediately enjoyed a two-hour siesta in clean sheets, a rare treat.

Now that I had time, well-being, and sanity, I was able to explore the considerable delights of the town, which had extensive stonework dating from the fourteenth to the eighteenth centuries. The little narrow streets with quaint balconies harked back to a different era, and the buildings lining them had now been reinvented into craft shops and hotels. In the historic twelfth-century Santa Juliana Collegiate Church I attended a high Mass, which was celebrated by an Italian priest who struggled a lot with the Spanish language. Afterward, I called into the hostel at the other end of town and met some brash young German walkers from a few days ago, but no one else I knew.

After a bite to eat in a friendly café on the edge of town, I went back to the posada. The quiet park in front of my room had been transformed into a salsa concert in full swing, with a stage, rides, food stalls, glittery costumes, and theatrical smoke. I discovered it was a fiesta in honor of the town's patron, Santa Juliana, whose feast was the next day. I was glued to the foot of the stage, soaking up the lights, colors, music, and dance that celebrated Cantabrian culture. I felt like I had been deprived of such joys on the ascetic Camino. Fatigue eventually forced me away—it had been a long day of many twists and turns. My reflection was short and sweet; sleep came easily.

Waking late, I stumbled down to a meager continental breakfast, not a fried egg in sight. Today, the actual feast day of Santa Juliana was another day of fiesta beginning with a solemn Mass and procession in her honor. The cobbled streets leading up to the church were filled with brightly colored traditional dresses and groups of men carrying life-size statues, including ones of Saint Juliana. A great group of clergy and acolytes in robes and lace added to the drama. I had never seen such pomp and pageantry: the elaborate costumes, the marching bands, the banners and flags, a huge standard bearing the saint's image, all topped off with fireworks.

Just before Mass I spotted my friend Willy from a few days ago coming into town enveloped in plastic from the rain. I was delighted to see him, and we chatted briefly in our unique sign language before he had to go on. "We'll have a beer in Finisterre at the Camino's end," he shouted as he walked away. I was sad to see him go; it reinforced the fact that I was presently unable to walk. I was left alone with little to do for the rest of the day, especially after the morning's excitement. The boarding house offered no solace: with the bedroom's dull floral print and windows that opened to brick walls, I could have been anywhere in the world.

Since the afternoon was completely rained out, I decided to walk the short distance out of town to the zoo as a distraction. I also wanted to test how my feet were holding up and, promisingly, they seemed better. I felt curiously unbalanced walking on a road without my pack, like a fundamental part of me was missing. The rain was bouncing off the road, and the vegetation sagged under its weight. Located on the side of a ravine, the zoo was home to hundreds of species, and under a canopy of thick vegetation.

However, with the dismal day, all the animals looked pathetic and miserable, which didn't help my mood much. I made a beeline for the brown bear enclosure to admire the great North American beasts.

One of them kept making desperate attempts to escape, swinging up the side of the enclosure. It was distressing to see the enforced captivity of a wild creature in a steel cage. Even worse, the other bears had simply given in to immobility, apathetically resigned to their fate.

The lethargic bears struck me as an image for Donal's depression. Unable to cope, both had tuned out of the world and into an alternate reality. I remember when things had come to a head some twenty years ago and I took time off from my job in England to help my brother. Taking on too much, ignoring accumulated stress, and not having an emotional safety valve had created an emergency situation for him. Even getting the help of a specialist and medication did little to take the edge off it. It was the beginning of a two-decade drift that scarcely registered initially, but ossified over time and gradually eroded the space for healthy living.

It was painful for me to watch this happen to a person I loved while knowing that solutions were possible. I and many of my siblings, some of them experienced health professionals, were powerless to act. We could only watch this tragedy unfold with horror. I had written before that Donal "drowned in a pool full of lifeguards,"[69] and it was utterly devastating to be left as a rescuer with a slack rope, all attempts having failed. Particularly cruel was that the summer before his death, Donal miraculously appeared to be back to his positive self and on the mend. But instead of recovery, this was a common warning sign of imminent suicide that should

Accompanying someone who's at risk from suicide sorely tests your patience, ingenuity, mental health, and discernment. Even after being a good listener, taking a nonjudgmental stance, and encouraging the person to seek help, one feels anguish in watching how mental illness can disable a person's coping strategies. Finally, there is the cruel irony of how an apparent improvement can actually be a warning signal. The concept of balance and being wary of extremes can be useful in interpreting this complex issue.

have set off alarm bells. I so much wanted to believe that the tide was turning and that rescue was on its way. Blinded by intense desire, I misread the signs and reaped a harvest of regrets. I realized now, on a rainy hillside in Santillana del Mar, that letting go of the terrorism of the "shoulds" and allowing self-forgiveness was the journey I needed to walk. I still had a ways to go.

The tropical butterfly house I stumbled upon next was a joy though, with its hot and steamy climate. I was surrounded by thousands of delicate furry wings flying over and around me, many landing on my clothes. Turquoise, gold, and yellow wings of impossible fragility flew playfully around a host of tropical plants—I found out later that one of the more striking butterflies that had brown wings and beige-colored edges was called the Mourning Cloak. I felt like I had been transported to a parallel dream world of vivid color, delicacy, and beauty. The Camino appeared hard, drab, and uninviting in contrast. I fantasized about remaining wrapped in this sultry cocoon, immobile and safe, but like the bears, I knew this was not the place for me. The only bars preventing me from escape were those in my own head: fears, exaggerations, and doubts. The idea of giving up preyed on my mind, but I knew I had to act against it.

The lethargy of the bears, the seductive deception of Donal's seeming recovery, and now my own resignation at another setback all seemed to point toward a subtle but destructive negativity. Depression has an insidious reasoning that justifies inactivity, withdrawal, and poisonous rumination. You must act against these instincts,

> When emotions of negativity, spiritual dryness, and depression feel overwhelming, we must *act against* them, better known as *agere contra*. Instead of waiting out the storm of emotions, Ignatius calls us to take positive steps and get back on track.

get going, engage, and crawl out from under the cloud, even though it feels like the opposite of what you want to do. Rather than waiting until you feel good, you must act, regardless of the feelings. Ignatius of Loyola knew this counterintuitive dynamic well. Sometimes he had to galvanize himself into action, digging deep in difficult moments, resisting easy solutions, and getting back on track. Ignatius called this challenging approach "acting against":[70] when you're in a rut, lazy, or in desolation, you have to act against the way you feel and take decisive steps to get back on course. I really wished that Donal could have profited from this wisdom, to act against his demons, face down the deceptions, and make those crucial, courageous decisions. I wanted him to be a free butterfly and not a caged bear, but he wasn't able to make the transformation for a whole host of reasons, many beyond his control. I needed to forgive him too.

The experience crystallized my desire to get back on the trail the next day. I had to act against an encroaching negativity that tempted me to surrender and give in. Sitting around would not address the situation, but walking carefully would. I decided to do whatever distance I could reasonably do the next day, starting off slowly and observing my limits. I was glad for the blessings of a day of reflection;[71] even though challenging, I had a new clarity and focus. It became increasingly clear that I had to learn a few lessons about taking it easy, not walking in the heat, and lowering expectations.

# 7

# Get out of Jail

It wasn't even light when I walked out of Santillana, I was so anxious to get moving. The last two days seemed like a dark chapter of blisters and boarding houses that I wanted to forget. With every step my heart lifted; I was glad to be back on the road again, a pilgrim. I felt free and alive, the blisters healed and forgotten. I needed to believe this was a new start, getting over the indignity of being immobilized. Fortunately, it was an easy, flat-road walk, and the big mountains of the Basque Country were a distant memory. It started to rain though, drizzling at first and then coming down more consistently. I was forced to dig out my luminous red cape, which the wind instantly made into a sail. With the clouds and weather down, it was a dull landscape, the telegraph poles scraping a low grey sky.

Once again I hadn't managed to get any breakfast before I left, so I was quickly running on empty. I walked on through several drab Cantabrian villages that showed no sign of life. With the rain dripping off my cape, I made it to an unremarkable coffee shop in a town called Cóbreces around nine in the morning and was amazed to meet the stroppy Spanish woman of the "lost" crisis a few days earlier and a Dutch guy who had been there too. I was glad to see some familiar faces and be among friends. Normally I walked alone, but that day I needed company. We ordered some café con leche, toast, and eggs and sat in the half-light by the door as the rain continued to fall outside.

My companions had just arisen from a nearby hostel and were having a leisurely morning. As we caught up, I recounted the story of my adventures so far: my forced stay in Santillana del Mar and having to take the bus. Immediately I could tell they weren't impressed. In fact, the Spanish woman had a bit of an edge to her voice as she chastised me for deviating from the Camino and taking shortcuts. It was the "Camino purist" ethic[72] in its classic form, and I found myself reacting to her hostility. I was a bit taken aback—I felt some defensiveness and frustration at being challenged, but mostly I felt knocked off my game. I realized I had to change strategy rapidly to avoid getting pulled into her agenda.[73] She became more strident, insisting I withdraw from the Camino, that I wasn't experienced enough, and that I would not be able to finish it. I couldn't believe what I was hearing from a fellow pilgrim.

Instinctively, I knew I had to dig deep[74] to maintain my balance and fend off this attack, which came at a low moment. After taking a moment to collect myself, conscious that I did not want to react in a similarly angry way, I replied, "There are many different Caminos," an intriguing phrase I had heard used by Camino walkers to describe the uniqueness of each person's journey. I had to repeat this several times, like a broken record, to shake her off her evangelical pedestal.

> St. Ignatius had an interesting metaphor for the way our "enemies" attack us. He compared them to army commanders examining a fortress and attacking its weakest spot. Our enemy will aim where he finds us most vulnerable, and he won't be attacking head on. We need to be aware of our weaknesses and shore these up when in trouble.

To add salt to the wound, the Dutch guy chipped in that he thought something was wrong with my shoes—he had noticed my right foot turning outwards when he was walking behind me a few days previously. I thanked him for this observation (which was to prove useful later). Eventually we came to a conversational impasse from a lack of common ground. They donned their rain gear and headed off for San Vincente, some 15 kilometers away. I was glad they were gone, but it took a while to shake off the resentment and be free of it.[75] I had a *pan dulce* (sweet bread) and an extra coffee to calm down, feeling shaken by this unexpected emotional tsunami.

Galvanizing myself into action, I had a look around the rest of the town, which was only a thin strip of buildings on the side of a hill. One building stood out immediately though, a freshly painted Cistercian abbey, the Abadía de Santa María de Viaceli. I was used to churches and abbeys being deserted, but on inspecting the notice board, I discovered that there was an active community of about thirty monks there and that midmorning prayer was in progress. A sign on the door said "Do not enter during prayer times," but I considered this a spiritual emergency, given the morning I had had. I snuck (noisily with my rucksack) into the Cistercians' inner sanctum—thankfully the monks and other people praying gave me only the slightest of glances. The chapel was a welcome refuge of light and warmth on what had been a mean, wet day. Even though I couldn't follow the prayers, being there was enough. I gave thanks for surviving my hardest test yet and for the hard-won wisdom. As I came out, the rain had stopped, and hope sprung anew in my heart: I was still on course to Santiago despite the obstacles.

I took off my rain cape as the sun struggled out from its leaden prison. I slipped into that lovely but elusive rhythm that makes walking effortless, and began to process what had happened after that difficult morning. Gradually things swam back into focus and my peace returned.[76] Ironically, the earlier conflict had fired my determination to walk at my own pace, which was "in a relaxed manner."[77] I purposefully took my time and enjoyed every detail, even though my feet began to hurt again. Fortunately I was close to Comillas, my destination for the day, and I could see the coast again. Tramping along the Bay of Biscay, I breathed deeply and loved being alive.

That day, however, the town's famous crescent beach was damp and uninviting. I entered the historic and picturesque town of Comillas through the main plaza, and then I came upon a cemetery protected by an imposing marble angel. Over at the tourist office, a woman kindly let me leave my rucksack in her office since the hostel wasn't open yet. After eating *huevos*

> Walking can be an effective way to connect with God and to remind you that you are always a pilgrim. In the next few days, try walking and wandering, praying with what emerges, and breathing in God's presence as you stroll. Notice what comes up in you in terms of feelings, desires, and decisions.

*revueltos*, a local dish of fried eggs and bacon, in a café seemingly hewn from the sandstone rock, I set about exploring this Roman town.

Comillas is rich in history with different layers of civilization written into its very walls. I was taken with the main church, San Cristóbal, the seventeenth-century exterior of which was dramatically crumbling away to reveal a variety of stone and brick surfaces. I continued my architectural stroll around the pretentious neo-Gothic Palacio de Sobrellano, the cemetery with the grim exterminator angel, and Gaudí's folly, El Capricho de Gaudí, a beautiful Arabesque-style building with a mix of bizarre shapes and styles. As the sun descended, I walked around the scenic port and wondered at some ominously high mountains on the horizon.

I raced back to the hostel for its 4 p.m. opening, but a queue had already formed. The hostel was a rugged, square stone building, and the windows had obviously been added recently to what would have been blank walls. I discovered the hostel had been the town's eighteenth-century jail—which I would have cause to remember later.

Lining up for an albergue bed is a great leveler; people naturally fall into conversation with one another. I greeted the pilgrim behind me, and within a few minutes we were talking like intimates. He was a Spanish priest who worked in Peru. Miguel had been trained by the Jesuits in Madrid, so we had a lot of common ground right away. He asked me if I had celebrated Mass that day (I hadn't) and invited me to accompany him to the local church to ask if we could concelebrate. Ditching my rucksack on a bed, I happily went with him.

Within minutes we were back at the church of San Cristóbal (of the crumbling walls), and as it was the feast day of their patron, San Pedro el Pescador, the pews were packed. We walked up the main aisle, and I was captivated by the huge pillars that soared up into a Gothic ceiling. I admired Miguel's confidence as he strode into the sacristy and presented us as a liturgical team. The parish priest seemed happy at the offer and asked us to lead the whole evening's Mass. The next thing I knew, Miguel was dividing up the liturgical tasks, inviting me to preach the homily on the Gospel. I balked at this, knowing my Spanish, while good, would not stretch to that without serious preparation.

In the end Miguel was the main celebrant, and I read the Gospel. I knew Miguel was the right man for preaching when I saw him hold the whole congregation in rapt attention, effortlessly ad-libbing like an old hand. I had a vision of St. Peter evangelizing the Gentiles, full of zeal and conviction, such was his passion and presence. Just when I thought all was over, there was a eucharistic procession around the village, complete with a band, singers, and dancers. Miguel and I were the principal dignitaries. Every few minutes the procession would stop in the thronged village square, and the dancers would twirl as fireworks were set off. It was then that I caught the eyes of some of our fellow pilgrims from the hostel, who were incredulous at our presence there. Afterward Miguel and I had a simple meal of fried mackerel and bread with a glass of wine as we unwound from a hectic day. On the way back to the hostel we paused, just as the sun was setting over the ocean, by a stone cross set high above the town. I was touched by a feeling of beauty and heartrending sadness. I thought of how Donal would have loved to share this moment, this "spiritual peak."

I was making a mess out of my unpacking as I wearily sought to silently untangle my gear on a top bunk. Three other hikers were sleeping nearby, so I brought my rucksack out to the common room so as not to disturb them. Just as I was heading back to the bedroom, there was a knock on the hostel door. The warden had gone home for the night, but feeling brave, I opened it to the curious sight of a young man clutching a bike, his arm held by a policeman. The young guy, who was called José, was in cycling shorts with his arm bleeding and bike damaged. I initially thought José was a prisoner being taken by the police into custody (we were in the old jail after all). The truth was less dramatic: José had arrived late into town and had asked the police for help. They brought him to the hostel and, being a little overly officious, insisted that he register and pay for a room.

I knew I should get José inside fast, so I helped him wheel in his old-style racing bike. Tiptoeing around the now almost-full hostel, I got him a free bed. Back in the common room I began telling him about my police-prisoner misperception, and we both began to laugh at the absurdity of it all. Soon, we were reduced to hysterical snorts and wheezes. Eventually we said good night, and I wished him well on his goal to get to Santiago in five days. He reminded me a lot of Robert Powell from the film *Jesus of Nazareth*.

That night as I did my usual Review of the Day, I was struck by what an outstanding day it had turned into. There were so many good things, including the improving weather, the beauty of Comillas, meeting Miguel, the special Mass and procession, and

> The Examen, a five-step review of our day, allows us to see our life through God's eyes so we're able to see the gifts and blessings of the day. Where have you noticed God's presence in your day?

finally, encountering José. Most significant, however, was how I hadn't let the Spanish woman get to me or ruin my day. With some help from Ignatius I was able to see the day through God's eyes, as a gift. I could even look compassionately on the Spanish woman and reinterpret what could have been a toxic situation. Far from ruining my day, it had focused me, energized my quest to do the Camino my way, and brought me all sorts of unexpected rewards—friends, community, and significant experiences.

This warm feeling evaporated as I woke up washed out and haggard. I hadn't slept a wink due to the guy opposite me snoring loudly. He had roared and receded like waves on a pebble beach. I had tried a few tricks, like whistling and coughing loudly, but nothing worked. Tired and cranky, I found myself packing my things beside the snorer during the morning exodus. My anger was ratcheting up to confront him when he turned and disarmed me with a smile. Completely oblivious to the nocturnal frustrations he had caused, he was bright as a button. Instead, I was the one who was still carrying the frustration. His infectious enthusiasm brightened my day.

I set off just after six, first out of the hostel, wanting to be alone in nature. It was another lovely morning, the sky roseate, though it felt cool—ideal walking weather. I skirted some tidal estuaries first, the low water revealing the silty contours and fingers of the river basins. Then I wound my way up into the Cantabrian hills, which reflected shades of green, blue, and grey. As I came down a narrow rutted track,

I met a grim-looking farmer with a sickle over his shoulder. Introducing himself as Francisco, he gave me a rundown on horses, feed, the harvest, and fishing. I marveled again at the way walking connected me to him and to the land.

I had already walked more than ten kilometers and was hungry. I didn't come across a café until I reached San Vincente, a lovely town built around a bay, accessible by a long stone causeway. As I sat outside a café, I spotted a familiar rickety bike and rider. I greeted José, the guy from the hostel the previous night. He joined me for coffee, and we laughed again over the events of the night before. We began talking about our lives and about philosophy, film, and theories on life. Totally engaged, I forgot about being competitive or getting ahead on the Camino—the human connection was much more important. We were living in the moment and being present to each other, and this spontaneous and flowing conversation lived on in my memory as a "hearts on fire"[78] experience. I was happy to find out later that José did make it all the way to Santiago on his beat-up bike.

Later that day I bumped into my priest friend, Miguel, who was now in the company of a Frenchman, Lionel, and two young sisters from California, Liz and Virginia. Unaccustomed to walking with others, it took me a while to relax and see this as a gift too—the fun of walking as a group. I couldn't help noticing that Lionel was carrying a super slim day pack. Intrigued, I discovered he was on a "Camino-plus" deal whereby his bag was carried for him, his lunches were pre-packed, and he slept in pre-booked hotel rooms. This news took a bit of getting used to, but it was an inevitable part of marketing that opened up the Camino to all types of walkers. I was glad that he was experiencing the Way anyhow, though glad, too, of my own freely chosen traditional "pilgrim" method. Maybe I really was becoming less judgmental and more accepting.

We stopped for lunch at a country bar, chasing the chickens from the door as we entered. Lunch was a noisy affair with the television blaring behind us and the conversation animated by several beers. At the table, it was evident how different all the cultures present were. For example, the American women treated the Camino like a holiday, Lionel wanted a relaxing hike, and Miguel saw it as a serious pilgrimage. Afterward we went our separate ways, the sisters returning home, and I was alone again. I breathed a sigh of relief back on the road—it had been delightful company but tough going for a solitary pilgrim.

Uncharacteristically, I found myself walking in the heat of the afternoon with a new challenge: trekking through a working quarry layered in white sand, which created a blinding glare and made walking difficult. The trail led up a long concrete lane that ran almost vertically uphill and had me gasping. It was late afternoon by the time I arrived in Pesues, a village some four kilometers from Unquera, my intended destination. After trying a few side roads, I could no longer see any yellow arrows and realized I was lost. Retracing my steps, I went back to the plaza and asked a group of teenagers playing Spanish guitars in a bus shelter for directions. Graciously they told me, and I hung around as they resumed singing, aware of their considerable talent. I applauded them to show my support and appreciation. I couldn't help mentioning that I, too, played guitar; immediately one young guy offered me his. I played the U2 song "With or Without You," and then passed the guitar back. We took turns playing different songs until we hit on the ideal configuration: I would sing classic rock songs in English and the young guy would accompany me on guitar. We went through "Sweet Home Alabama," "Stairway to Heaven," "Hotel California," and many others. Even though we barely spoke a word to each other, we had a glorious hour of sharing music and song. It was another memorable Camino moment, spontaneous and inclusive.

Dusk was falling as we finished, and I began to look for accommodation. My two friends Miguel and Lionel appeared out of the gloom. It turned out Lionel had a reservation in the two-star hotel on the main road, and he invited us to stay there too. Done in as I was, I decided to take up the offer, though Miguel grumbled for a while before accepting. Safely tucked in bed, I realized it had been another great day, full of adventure, connections, and people. I was grateful; maybe I was getting this Camino "thing."

# 8

# Soul Crisis

The Hotel Baviera in Pesues was not exactly plush—the rooms were more like tin boxes fitted out with iron furniture and linoleum. A grey dawn filtered through the metal shutters, and a slam jolted me into consciousness. The doors rattled and banged around me as other guests, mainly hikers, performed their morning ablutions. Packing was easy with such scant belongings, and like a refugee I had learned to leave everything ready for a quick exit. After a hurried wash I went downstairs for a meager breakfast, joining Lionel and Miguel, my two friends from the day before. They wanted to set a tough pace, and sensing my reluctance, arranged a rendezvous for later that night. I had a bad feeling about my increasingly painful right foot and felt relieved watching them go.

Though I was hobbling somewhat, I was happy to be alone on the road again. I looked a little like a camel with my washed clothes pinned to my pack to dry, a trick I learned from the Internet. I headed downhill on a broad multi-lane road toward the sleepy town of Unquera as the sun rose into a flawless azure sky. The town spread out along the river Deva and was dominated by a hill on the north side. By the time I reached the outskirts of Unquera some forty minutes later, I was limping and in considerable pain and knew I was in trouble. The planned rendezvous with my friends wasn't going to happen. I was crestfallen—these recurring problems seemed insurmountable, a crushing, dispiriting burden.

Frankly, I had been ignoring problems with this foot all along. My Dutch friend had drawn attention to this, which explained all the blisters and pain. I suspected poor arch support in my shoes, a structural issue that, though hidden, was now obvious. Disconsolate, I wanted to give up, to throw myself on the ground and weep. I felt like such a failure, especially as this was the third such crisis. Maybe this trip was doomed or there was something fundamentally wrong with me. I felt the withering hand of worthlessness and despair on my shoulder. I had a sudden flash of insight into what Donal must have felt: the crushing burden of repeated failure, the numbing bleakness of seeing only one way out. Remembering how this shadow gradually eclipsed my brother reminded me how easily darkness can dominate.

Ignatius of Loyola also had the experience of his life becoming unbearable. I had been amazed to read that Ignatius, renowned saint and mystic, was once on the verge of suicide. As part of his transformation from courtier to pilgrim, he went through a harsh process of self-denial and fasting, recklessly adopting extreme penitential measures. His

> Desolation is an uneasy feeling that sweeps up doubts, fears, restlessness, and temptation. We feel farthest away from God during this period, and it is a sign that something is out of balance. Desolation can sweep us away through euphoric and transitory feelings, which can land us in trouble.

self-contempt and obsessive scruples were such that he considered throwing himself out a window in Manresa to end his mental anguish. Clearly in the grip of great depression, his false perfectionism brought him to the verge of self-destruction. I had read an article by Ignatian scholar Joseph Munitiz, who argued that clinical depression was the overriding cause and that Ignatius wasn't acting from spiritual desolation, which looks very similar.[79] Significantly, the extremes of depression and attempted suicide did force him to face reality (that he was on the cusp of starvation) and to act decisively against this damaging negativity (by abandoning excesses and banning scrupulosity). Additionally, he was able to spiritually discern that the disgust he was feeling about his new reformed lifestyle and the temptation to abandon it was the action of the bad spirit.[80] He experienced this as feelings of desolation, working to undo the progress he had made.

How I wished that Donal could have used this same reflective ability to avoid suicide. Obviously depression was a mitigating factor and had clouded his perception, as it had Ignatius's. However, Ignatius's spiritual insights would have been useful in recognizing destructive impulses (e.g., isolation, stress) and distinguishing them from those that were genuinely life-giving. Ignatius's whole system of reflection and discernment was precisely about making good decisions. During this inner turmoil we see Ignatius's process develop: reflecting on his emotions, judging which emotions are not genuinely good, and then making life-affirming decisions (in his case, resuming eating and not harming himself). It is a profound but practical spirituality that all Jesuits learn. Sadly, I had tried to teach some of this discernment to my troubled brother, but even fraternal bonds are not strong enough to deal with such powerful forces.

I was experiencing a similar emotional morass here in Unquera as I paced the riverbank. In refusing to accept the injury (avoiding reality) and procrastinating, I was undermining the reflective process. I was tempted to pack it all in and go home, or to walk on and ignore the foot pain, or even take some painkillers to make it go away. After a prolonged struggle, I felt some freedom and openness creep in, in seeking help. I was praying to make the best decision, not to give in to an easy fix that could be costly in the long run. It made sense to take a detour to fix my foot, but I had a sense of failure and embarrassment about breaking off the Camino again.

Imprisoned by guilt, I felt I was letting everyone down, including Donal. Was this actually a good basis for making a decision though? The strength of the conflicting emotions was paralyzing me. I thought of Ignatius lying on his sixteenth-century sickbed agonizing over the broken leg that had ended his military career. Interestingly, he had found the answer within himself, being able to go deeper than his superficial feelings and arriving at a place of

> Ignatius calls us to cultivate indifference, a passionate desire to place God above all other things. With this approach, we're open to receiving gifts—wealth or material things—or letting them go, depending on what God wants. When we're indifferent, we're present in each moment, with our hearts and hands open to God's call, and free to make wise choices.

peace. He later formulated this as "indifference."[81] I needed some of this now.

In a flash of insight I decided I would get the injury sorted out properly, regardless of my surface emotions and feelings. I resolved to go to the nearby city of Oviedo to get treatment and then rest for a while to allow my foot to heal. With time running out, I had to get it right to be able to walk into Santiago. I studied Oviedo on the map: an hour away, it was a big city but located on another Camino route, the Primitivo. I rang my Jesuit friend José in Burgos, and he organized my stay with the Jesuit community in Oviedo. Shortly it was all arranged, and I was at peace again, having coffee and waiting for the bus.

I took a stroll along the Deva River and admired the terracotta-roofed town houses opposite. The river was like glass, moving effortlessly by. Not for the first time, I wondered where this Camino was taking me. Taking a detour from the main Camino and being out of action for a while was hard medicine. I hoped to rejoin the walk soon, injury free and with renewed energy. I prayed to be open to what Oviedo would bring, that I would be well received and that I would get the necessary help. I really wanted to be restored so that in memory of Donal I could finish my quest—the only thing that mattered.

Within a few minutes I was on the bus for Oviedo and sitting in air-conditioned luxury. I marveled at how the distance of a whole day's walking could be effortlessly achieved in minutes—no wonder it felt like cheating! Out of habit I scoured the mountains for hikers but could see none. I appreciated every little thing, especially the spectacular scenery passing my window. I was now in another province, Asturias (having already walked through the Basque Country and Cantabria), and the imposing Picos de Europa were on my left. The rugged limestone and glaciated surfaces gave them an unreal quality; they were so steep and so tightly packed together. I read that there were bears and wolves there, so remote and extensive was the park. I had intended to get some sleep, but the thrilling view wouldn't allow it. *This is an unexpected gift*, I thought, warming up to this new adventure.

The bus pulled into Oviedo around noon, and out of habit, the first thing I did was make up a chorizo sandwich on a sunny park bench. Everything seemed charged with possibility in the dazzling sunlight. The Jesuit residence on Doctor Casal Street was so close that, despite my injury, I was able to walk there. Seeing this exotic city's amalgam of traffic, plazas, cafés, and apartments for the first time was intoxicating. Excited, I asked a man to take a photo of me. A very friendly guy, he told me he was from Cuba and had only temporary residence in Spain. We traded stories about how we had gotten here; I told him I would like to go to Cuba one day, and we parted laughing. It seemed the Camino magic hadn't left me. On Doctor Casal Street the buildings were tall and imposing, mainly apartment blocks with a church on the corner. I wondered what the welcome would be.

To my relief, Brother José Manuel, who met me, was the epitome of hospitality. I was given a room on the sixth floor and took a moment to settle in. Not for the first time, I was so grateful for the Jesuit network and its ready hospitality across the world. At that stage I felt weary but waited for lunch to meet the others in the community. They were relatively young and very welcoming, especially when they realized I spoke some Spanish. Afterward, I had a much-needed siesta, and then José Manuel brought me to the commercial district. It turned out that he was a self-styled expert in foot problems and knew exactly where to go. I marveled at the serendipity of this. We went to an orthotic specialist who knew José Manuel personally. She measured my feet and showed me various insoles but didn't have anything in my size. After much searching, we finally found a pharmacist who had the right size. We left the shop triumphant, the new insoles fitted, and with a packet of anti-inflammatories just in case. Even my foot seemed to feel better already. I felt indebted to José Manuel for his persistence and constant generosity to me, a virtual stranger.

After a dinner of monkfish, vegetables, and sliced potatoes, one of the Jesuit priests invited me to evening Mass at the nearby Sagrado Corazón (Sacred Heart) Church. The church facade was made out of warm limestone and red brick, reflecting the name. Inside was packed and had a strong community feel. It was the feast of the Sacred Heart of Jesus,[82] which meant a glorious combination of Mass, the rosary, recital of the novena prayer, and then exposition after Mass. Seeing the sea of faces bowed in adoration, I was struck by the variety of different paths to God. I had been finding God in the erratic nature of the road, while here they were finding God in an ancient devotion. I felt so deeply grateful for all that the Camino had given me; I had experienced God's providence and protective care. With rising emotion I felt that Donal, no matter the tragedy of his life and death, could never be outside this encompassing love of the Sacred Heart.[83] I felt heartened by this insight on my temporarily stalled mission.

A huge party was in full swing in the city when I returned home. One could be forgiven for thinking that the Spanish have one fiesta after another, given my experience in the last few days. Seeing the fireworks from the rooftop that night, I instinctively reviewed the highlights of the day. I had much to be grateful for: I had received food and shelter, I had great Jesuit companions around me, and I had solved my foot problem, all in one fell swoop. Could this finally be the new start that I was looking for?

I sank into bed for some long-overdue rest. Unconsciousness reigned until suddenly something had a grip on me. I felt the panic rise. I was trapped, pinned to the bed, and couldn't get free no matter how hard I tried. Frightened, I struggled even harder to no avail. With a shock I realized I was almost paralyzed. It was creeping through my organs, and I was slowly dying. I toyed with giving in, sliding into oblivion, but something held me back. *I'm not ready to die, I want to live!* was my urgent thought. I thrashed and raged at the hidden chains. Then consciousness raced in, and I woke up in a sweat from the dream's hold. It took me some time to work out where I was, and gradually I sat up.

The morning sun struggled to enter the double layer of curtain and blinds, rendering the sunlight a murky brown. I was in Oviedo, in the ancient kingdom of Asturias, and I was alive. I came to with some incredulity, remembering the eventful last few days. Miraculously, I was still on the Camino and relatively intact, in spite of the events that had conspired to throw me off course. The kindness of the community here had saved me in many different ways, especially in getting my foot problem sorted and giving me a shot at getting to Santiago. Gratitude overcame me like a warm glow. I had been given yet another chance when all seemed lost.

I had the luxury of a day off and time to reflect, of which Ignatius would have approved.[84] There was also a beautiful city to explore. I found the Gothic Cathedral of San Salvador impressive, but it was the Cámara Santa, an interior treasure room, that was really intriguing. The room contained the Shroud of Oviedo, the bloodstained cloth that reputedly was wrapped around Christ's head in the tomb. It was a symbol for suffering and transition—*the cost of love*, I thought.

> St. Ignatius recommended removing ourselves from distractions and noise to better hear God's voice. Often, this can be heard in the peace and quiet of nature, a chapel, or a quiet room. It's in our nature to recognize God's presence within us, but we need time and space to cultivate this.

I mused about my own life as a series of little deaths and new beginnings, whether it was changing careers, joining the Jesuits, going to a new country (Colombia and Canada), or gaining hard-won lessons and insights. The hardest thing I had ever faced though, was scraping myself back together after the devastating loss of Donal to suicide. Suicide had totally reconfigured everything for me: relationships, sureties, my worldview, faith, the very ground on which I stood. The grief process after suicide was terrifying, unlike any other. There was a shocking brutality in the manner of his death. I was left with all these unanswered questions—the persistent "why?" and "what did I do wrong?" among others. I felt I had failed Donal in not being vigilant enough and had missed some key warning signs. The result was insidious burdens of guilt and remorse. I tried to stagger on normally, but it became increasingly impossible to cope under the crushing weight. It was only when I reached the limit of my abilities and coping strategies that change occurred. I was forced to reach beyond my comfort zone, beyond even the normal supports of friends and counseling. Ironically, it was my belief in the spiritual, recast in the fire of suffering, that was key to providing meaning and support in this darkest of processes.

I obsessed about Jesus' moment on the cross when he faces awful agony and feels that God, his Father, has abandoned him.[85] From my own suffering I felt the same sense of desertion. For Jesus, the absence of pleasant feelings or comforting presence didn't mean God was absent. I had to face up to this paradoxical truth too. It was cold comfort, but Ignatius of Loyola would have agreed with this as well. Superficial feelings aren't important in staying the course. What's important is managing to persevere as Jesus did through the pain. As a Jesuit, it was a challenge to blindly hang on, a broken heart in search of healing.

Applying the Jesuit catchphrase "finding God in all things" seemed both repulsive and intriguing when facing a suicide. For the longest time I blamed God, an easy target for my anger. I had this persistent dream-like image where I held my brother's body in my arms up to God and howled in anger and recrimination. There was no answer. Was God uncaring or was he unable to act? The image did, however, expose some of my naive beliefs: that God would protect me from bad things and that God was responsible for everything that occurred.[86] Before I could let God off the hook though, I had to pass through the purifying furnace of grief. It was a blind roller-coaster ride, guaranteed to expel false pride and self-reliance. Who was I to question God or hold him accountable? The process helped reshape my faith, bringing about a new understanding. Central to it were humility and gratitude, seeing everything as a gift. Unfortunately, it nearly took my mind, too, the ravages of soul pain exacting a terrible cost. I knew early on I had to get help.

A few years ago something com-
pelled[87] me to seek a support group.
Initially I joined a depression group by
mistake but was eventually steered
toward a suicide-bereavement group,
Console,[88] which was to become my
home. Initially my anxiety was
high—would I be judged for what
happened to Donal? Would I be
labeled too, or seen as being at risk?

> Sometimes prayer is not enough, and you have to do something concrete and challenging to break out of a rut. Joining a support group, seeking professional help, talking to a friend, helping someone else, or making small, positive steps each day can help lead you to a better place.

Committed to find some support, I joined a small group of fairly
normal-looking people in north Dublin one blustery autumn
evening. The head of the organization, Paul Kelly, spoke courageously
about losing his sister, Sharon, and why he had set up Console. It gave
me courage, and like the others I slowly found my voice over the next
few weeks.

The stories people unleashed were savage and excruciating. There
were tears and regrets and immeasurable heartache. Like ships in an
unmerciful storm we were all dashed onto the jagged rocks of grief.
We couldn't save anyone from his or her situation, but the bonds of
solidarity were such that we could survive the worst ravages together.
Just knowing someone was listening, who would listen without judgment, was an anchor. I came away from those meetings reeling from
the onslaught of tragedy but paradoxically renewed to have witnessed
such transparency. Most encouraging was realizing there was a profound healing process that eventually buoyed everyone to the surface,
a self-righting mechanism. Over time I could see people shift and
move, often not fully healed but managing to get by. Maybe God was
in this after all, just not in the way I expected.[89]

My day off in Oviedo had revealed much more than I bargained
for, yet it sharply defined the quest I was on and the answers I sought.

This was clearly a grief journey, and I was now conscious of the burden I carried and of the relief I searched for. I longed for the open road once more.

# 9

# The Road of Kings

I was having an identity crisis as a hiker on a day off from the trail. The Camino was so consuming that taking time away felt like cheating. Yet here I was in Oviedo, in northwest Spain, holed up in an apartment away from my originally planned route, and significantly behind on my itinerary. Far from the frantic hurry of peregrinos (pilgrims), I was relaxing and resting my tired legs and muscles, fortified by my new insoles. Yet somehow I couldn't enjoy it. On the one hand, my body was telling me I needed time to heal and recuperate. On the other hand, my mind was strident: *You're off track. This is wasted time; you will surely pay for this.* Of course, there was some value in keeping on schedule, but I had to reflect more to discover what was important.

Trying to keep to the original plan did not seem to be wise, based on the injuries I had suffered. You are stretched on the Camino, of course, but I suspected I was ignoring my body's wisdom and forcing too hard a pace. Of course, hikers have to judge for themselves by listening to their bodies. I knew many people on the Camino learned this lesson the hard way, injuring themselves, being unable to continue, and having to return home prematurely.[90] My hunch was that, like me, people were allowing the head to dominate the body and suffering the consequences.

Ignatius of Loyola had some hard-won expertise in this area. He himself did great damage to his health with excessive fasts, prolonged pilgrimages, and scant regard for his body. He walked some incredible distances on foot, crisscrossing Europe as a poor pilgrim begging his way through Spain, France, and Italy. Originally thinking that he was doing all these great ascetical deeds for God, he slowly came to realize that this element of excessiveness was damaging, unhelpful, and not from God. Sometimes these penances were beneficial, but only up to a point. Gradually he discovered that he was called to a more balanced approach with regard to walking, fasting, and eating.

The insight he eventually came to was captured by the ingenious phrase "insofar as" (*tanto cuanto* in Spanish),[91] meaning that anything can be helpful and a way to God insofar as it genuinely does come from God and deepens one's humanity. This means examining decisions to see where they come from and lead toward to see whether they really are good (from God) or whether they are coming from the ego, from rigidity, from negativity, or even from self-hate. For example, my initial decision to walk more than twenty-five kilometers a day on the Camino was proving to be a painfully unrealistic goal and in need of some adjustment. I needed to let go of some destructive ideas in my head (the perfect walk) and adjust to the actual reality of my situation: frequent injuries, a reduced fitness level, and a need for more recuperation and rest. Surprisingly, taking it easy in the Jesuit apartment felt like a wise option, as it would directly help me with the goal of getting to Santiago. I felt the word stir my heart, the finish line almost within reach.

The Jesuit community in Oviedo had given me a warm welcome and made me feel very much at home. They understood the Camino well, several of the younger members having walked it. As the itinerant "pilgrim" guest, I really appreciated the atmosphere of trust and affection, which means a lot when you're away from home. I enjoyed an informal Asturian dinner that night of crab stew, salmon, blue cheese, and a local wine. We squeezed around a circular table with a solitary light suspended over it and lingered on after the meal, enjoying the fun. Like the Irish, there was a bit of *tomando el pelo* (leg pulling), and I was delighted to find that the Spanish allowed me to join in.

Strangely, I had a strong sense of Donal's presence at the table that night. He always loved being at the center of the fun, and his easy sense of humor attracted people to him. I found myself taking on the same role, personifying the best parts of him. This was a real gift to me, allowing for some much-needed levity to offset the grim elements of my quest. In a small way, I felt he was helping me put aside the burden of grief that night, and I benefited from this lighthearted escapism. This last night in Oviedo was poignant, as the Camino was calling. Providentially, Oviedo was at the start of another route, the *Camino Primitivo*, which would bring me directly to Santiago.

The next morning I woke feeling lousy, a pulsating headache wanting to bury me in the bed. Nursing my sore head, I groaned as I sat up, remembering that I had gone out cider-tasting the previous night. It seemed like such a great idea when one of the Jesuits, Fermín, invited me to a *sidería* (cider house) with some prayer-group friends. I thought I would make my apologies and go to bed early, but I got carried away in a passionate conversation about the Northern Ireland peace process. The waiter poured cider from above his head into a glass at knee height, and the cider was so aerated

It is important to realize that we are continually under the influence of good or bad spirits. Ignatius has various "rules of thumb" that highlight these influences. One of these rules says that if you make a decision while in consolation, or a free and balanced state (the good spirit), don't reverse it. Especially in times of desolation, when you are tempted by the bad spirit to think God has abandoned you, stick with a previously made good decision.

as a result that it tasted like champagne. *Why did I not stop after one glass?* I berated myself. I was feeling dreadful now—my whole body felt like taking a sick day. I forced myself out of the house and staggered onto the street, remembering Ignatius's rule of thumb about sticking to a previously made decision.[92] I had my new insoles and socks on for courage and was ready to begin again, though hampered by a fierce headache and dehydration.

Legend has it that King Alfonso II had a vision of stars that inspired him to walk this new Camino. I was operating from slightly less romantic principles that day. Alfonso II had constructed a church, San Julián de los Prados, in the ninth century, on the outskirts of the city, and I chose that as my official starting point. A UNESCO World Heritage Site, the church was more than one thousand years old, but the ochre, crimson, and yellow frescos were still startling to my bleary eyes. The effect was that of being enclosed in a red velvet picture book—the colors were so striking and the artwork went right up the walls. Alfonso II was a great defender of Asturias and also apparently the first pilgrim to walk to Santiago de Compostela. He built the cathedral there over the remains of the apostle James. Alfonso had created this Camino Primitivo (the "original" or "first road"), the classic route, which I would now be walking into Santiago. *This was where it all began*, I thought, *in the footsteps of kings, nobles, and pilgrims.*

Once I had cleared the suburbs on the Camino Primitivo proper, I started to feel a bit more human and even slightly regal as the hangover wore off. I regretted leaving my original Camino del Norte, but I needed this direct mountain route to get to Santiago on time. Again I felt like I was beginning a new chapter, as if all the previous walking had been just a preparation. As with every change, there were pros and cons: this route was much busier with less solitude but had better signs and hostels. The guidebook indicated there would be huge mountains and some intimidating rocky passes. Here, however, the

Camino looked every inch the medieval royal way: it was cut deeply into the earth, paved with cobbles, and meandered through fields with curves pleasing to the eye.

Once out of Oviedo it was refreshing to see the iconic flechas amarillas again, and soon I was striding out among fields, livestock, and the activity of farming. The undulating meadows, grassland, and chugging tractors reminded me of my home county of Fermanagh, renowned for its "basket of eggs" landscape and rich pastoral tapestry. There was something about being in the country that was refreshing and renewing—it lifted the heart and opened the soul to God. Now that my morning fog had worn off, I was elated to be on the road again without encumbrance. My attention turned outward, freed from the hangover's internal pain. The sight of a familiar red Massey Ferguson tractor reminded me of carefree summers on the farm before "the great sadness."[93] I remembered hay bales and tractor races with my brothers, a paradise of innocence before the storm. Memory restored my faith in the world; it was a glimpse of some future hope that all could be well again. It was invigorating to be walking earthy country lanes, seeing the mountains, feeling alive. Surely nothing could stop me now?

There was one difference I noticed, however.[94] I was going at my own pace, stopping when I felt like it, not rushing, and taking time to drink in the rural vista. I was finally learning to slow down and "smell the flowers." My hard-won experiential learning invited me to be in the present moment, to let go of agendas and expectations. I internalized this "mindfulness"[95] resolve by walking only ten kilometers on my first day back on the road. What I had assimilated from the last few weeks was not to push my limits, to listen to my body, and to be aware of the experience.[96] As a result, the world seemed to sparkle with possibility. My perception was bright and clear, and my sense of consolation and connectedness to God present in the world deepened. Could it be that I had made progress?

Despite taking my time and getting lost once, I got to the nondescript brick albergue fairly quickly. It was on the outskirts of a village, surrounded by fields. As it was around noon and I still had time until it opened, I went back to the bar I had passed along the road and had the cheap menu del día meal. I relished taking my time eating and enjoying the food, my new philosophy. I also met some other pilgrims, who tried to persuade me to walk further. Avoiding the temptation, I let them go, unconcerned about what they thought. Then I went back to the locked hostel and found some sleeping mats and had a cool improvised siesta on its shady porch. Afterward, feeling bored and wandering around the area, I came across an elderly woman seated outside her apartment with crutches beside her. Her face was kindly and lined but collapsed on one side. She explained that she had had a stroke and her mobility was reduced as a result. Her story relativized my own fairly minor complaints. A model of kindness, she told me I could get a key for the hostel back in the same bar.

I walked back to the bar for the key, avoiding the trap of frustration at all the back and forth, and let myself into the hostel, which was pretty dirty at first sight. It obviously hadn't been cleaned since the previous night, but on the upside, it was bright and airy. The other pilgrims started to arrive en masse: several Dutch hikers; a Spaniard; and a Frenchman, Anton, who was eighty years old (a former marathon runner I discovered), and his Belgian companion Frederick. I was thrilled to recognize Anuk, a Dutch woman, from the original group I had met my first week. Introductions were made, and we quickly became a community of pilgrims, helping everyone settle in and feel welcome.

After the flurry of showers and clothes washing, we enjoyed a long, mellow session of lounging on the balcony in the evening sun and talking about hostels, stages, and guidebooks—all that good pilgrim stuff. Sunset found us all sitting around the dinner table on the terrace at the nearby bar. The food—the staple steak and chips—was very agreeable, leaving us relaxed and content. From our terrace that overlooked a dusky valley, we were dazzled by a blazing sunset. This day had brought good companions, got me back on route, and reenergized my mission. Tearful behind my sunglasses, I thought to myself, *This is such an amazing life. I am so grateful for all this day brought. Thank God I was able to get out of bed this morning and not miss this.* Thanks to Ignatius, too, for his useful rule of thumb.

At dawn, a misty turquoise sunrise drew me out of bed and to a nearby stubbly field, contemplating.[97] Used to being the first one on the road, I let the others pass me this time as I took in the beauty. I felt God was communicating with me through this dawn. I was being invited to begin the day with gratitude and let the rest be.

I felt something shift within me—I was seeing the world born anew, made of light and dew. The country lane was a little piece of heaven, made of fields, lanes, and hedgerows, with all their attendant smells, sights, and sounds. Some sheep bleated out staccato accompaniment. I hardly noticed the time[98] go by, held in the moment. I only reluctantly stopped for café con leche to get some much-needed sustenance. All the other pilgrims had gone ahead of me now. I let them go, content to walk my own Camino.

Later I fell in with a Belgian pair: a father who had walked more than two thousand kilometers, literally from his front door, and his son, who had joined him in Oviedo. They planned to finish the

> Ignatian spirituality calls us to be contemplatives in action. This phrase helps describe the tension inherent in Ignatian spirituality: it is an active spirituality, one concerned with our daily life as we find God in all people, places, and things. But it is also contemplative, acknowledging our need for prayer as we reflect and try to tune in to God.

Camino together. However, the father was much fitter, all tanned muscles and technique, while the son lagged behind, his legs still white and his muscles soft. I said good-bye; they were going too fast for me. As they walked off into the early mist, I had a sense of fore-boding—the disparity between them seemed too great and the distance between them irreconcilable. I was to meet the son ten days later, his feet too damaged to walk. He was zoned out watching tele-vision, hell-bent on escapism as he despondently made arrangements to head home. I held them in my heart, their good desire for time together having been overcome by condition and circumstance.

By noon I had made it into the large country town of Grado, where I managed to get a welcome lunch and a Wi-Fi connection to check my e-mail. Setting off again, I could feel the heat build, especially as I climbed a steep rocky hill en route to the next village, El Fresno. This was only a taste of the famed Cantabrian Mountains, my last great barrier before Santiago. I tried not to think about what lay ahead.

As I stopped for a rest at a crossroads, I saw a young couple shelling runner beans beside me. They were so focused on their task they didn't notice me for some moments. I asked for directions, and they told me that there was a hostel up ahead, near the top of the next huge hill. I decided I could climb it if I had a siesta first, so I went into a newly cut hayfield and lay down for twenty minutes. Outdoor snoozes reveal a captivating view of the sky and clouds, notwithstand-ing the nefarious insect bites.

Refreshed, I labored up the hill in low gear, gasping at times. By the time I reached the top, my stomach was growling, and I ate some more peanuts and fruit from my bag. Though I found a welcome water fountain, I could see no sign of a hostel. I had no choice but to continue over the top and downhill. It was even steeper and more treacherous, a mix of rock and blue clay, and very hard on the legs. I was glad it wasn't wet or slippery though; a fall would have been all I needed.

When I arrived in the next village, I still couldn't find a hostel or bar. The first couple must have misdirected me, or I had misunderstood. There was no point in getting mad about it, so I gave them the benefit of the doubt,[99] believing they genuinely wanted to help me. I chalked it up and let it go.

> If you are ever in doubt about a person's motives, try one of Ignatius's rules of thumb. The saint said we should believe the best and give the person the benefit of the doubt. This is a good starting place, as we assume goodwill until proven otherwise.

However, it meant I had to walk several kilometers to the next hamlet, Escamplero. My feet were hurting at this stage, and I struggled to stay positive.

Desperate to avoid any more walking, I went into the only bar in town, not holding out much hope for a bed. Incredibly, when I asked, they offered a bed in their tiny albergue out back. I laughed to see it was actually a wooden garden shed with only four beds, the smallest hostel I had seen. I was, however, exceedingly grateful to lay down my pack and relax. There was a bitter, rank smell of creosote, but it felt like a palace through the glaze of my fatigue. I had some supper in the bar with a German couple who were vegetarians (unfortunately, by the time I discovered this, I had already ordered a meal of chorizo and bacon), and who spoke excellent English. They were vacationing on the Camino, looking for the most scenic parts, and were planning on doubling back to the coast again. I told them I was an Irish priest on the Camino but didn't tell them of my rather personal quest. We passed a pleasant meal together and my good humor came flooding back with food and rest.

Later, as I unpacked my bag, another hiker arrived in the shed-hostel: Pedro, a stocky, swarthy Spaniard. With such small quarters I wondered how we would get on, but thankfully we hit it off right away. Within half an hour we were sitting outside like kings on the flimsy garden furniture, having a beer together. We talked at length about schools, as we were both teachers. Inevitably, the conversation turned to the allure of the Camino, and he told me he was doing it for the fifth time, a stage every year. Evening was falling, and so was the temperature, and we began to notice the loud roaring of the calves in the field next to us. I explained to him about weaning, where the calf and cow are separated in the first year and how the noise of the calf crying for its mother would last all night. It was a bizarre and surreal nightfall, in a garden shed at the back of a bar, accompanied by a calf chorus. This day had brought some great things—I had had to let go of a certain amount, but it ended well. I knew I was back in Camino mode.

# 10
# Alone and on Foot

My new friend, Pedro, and I were up at 6 a.m. to witness a grey, over-cast morning, perfect for walking. Within minutes we had packed everything in our shoe box of a room and were ready for the road. We left some euros on the bed, as this hostel invited a voluntary contribution. The weaned calves that had kept us awake half the night were now grazing, quiet and innocent as lambs. Swinging on our packs, we took the cobbled road to Cornellana, over an hour's walk away, zipping up our jackets against the cold. I could see right away that Pedro was setting a stiff pace—he only had a week off and was determined to make the most of it. I wondered how long I could keep up; I decided I would stop when the going got too tough for me.

The path wound its way across several bridges over the Narcea River, famous for its salmon fishing, and Pedro pointed out fishing spots along the way. The river itself was intriguing: a mottled mix of shade and light, currents and eddies, smooth and rough water. A metaphor for life itself, the river tumbled and transformed, the essence of fluid motion, seeking a path around obstacles. For centuries the Atlantic salmon had made their way from the sea, running all sorts of gauntlets to spawn here, only to die soon after. I could picture the medieval stockades and barriers that were used to trap the fish—maybe pilgrims reaped the bounty at this very spot. It reminded me that I was engaged in my own uphill battle and would need some of the courage of the wild salmon and the fluidity of water.

I really wanted to see an eleventh-century Romanesque monastery called San Salvador on the outskirts of Cornellana, especially as there was an albergue housed in its walls. Having seen *The Way*,[100] I had romantic visions of pilgrims sleeping in the cloisters with cowled monks gliding by in silent meditation. I also wanted to catch up with my original walking companions whom I missed so much. The monastery, however, was a letdown. Nothing like what I was expecting. Part of the inner courtyard had been turned into a pilgrim hostel, but the rest was in a terrible state of disrepair. The facade was stained with storm water, and the building bulged as if it would burst apart. This piece of rich ecclesial patrimony, built almost a thousand years ago, was falling into ruin. Also, I didn't recognize any faces among the departing pilgrims.

The place distressed me greatly—something about that crumbling ruin reminded me of Donal's slide into despair. He, too, had slowly decayed over the years. I left at a run, Pedro following, anxious to get back to some of the Camino's natural beauty. I later read in the local paper that there was a plan to renovate this once great building, so at least it had some hope. I put the monastery out of my mind. In the town I stopped for the ubiquitous *café con leche y napolitana* (I had just discovered the napolitana, a puff pastry with a chocolate filling, which, though sugary, was a taste sensation) in a café, and regrettably said good-bye to the fast-walking Pedro. I felt a great fondness for his brusque friendship and gave thanks for the precious time we had spent together. In classic Camino fashion he was gone in an instant, and I knew we would not meet again, at least in this life.

Unwittingly, I took the wrong road out of town and found myself some two kilometers off course. Stubbornly refusing to retrace my steps, I took the advice of some locals to cut straight across country to rejoin the Camino. The only trouble was that I had to climb through a quarry up a steep hill. Energy-wise, it was a costly shortcut. At the top of the next hill, however, an upland meadow littered with big, round, golden bales rolled out before me. The smell of sweet harvest hay hit me first, bringing me right back to those halcyon childhood days helping my father mow the fields. A bodily memory of wholeness settled upon me, a memory of life before the grimy rains of grief and loss had sullied it. Rejuvenated, I toiled on alone for many kilometers, managing to temporarily forget my burdens, happy just to be alive and moving. I reflected on what a gift each day, each moment, was—this richness continually offered if one has the eyes for it.

I was reminded of Ignatius of Loyola and his journeys throughout Europe, all on foot and largely alone. He was the archetypal pilgrim and the source of much of my inspiration as a Jesuit. I had left my career in computers to follow this pilgrim dream. Just as with the Camino, that meant being out "on the road," exposed to whatever

> As I learned to accept that I wasn't in control of the Camino, I became freer and more open to God working through me. Fear and self-centeredness often don't allow God in. But when we let go and let God in, we feel a great liberation and sense of consolation.

ups or downs this path brought, but also learning to trust in God's providence and care. Ignatius had learned over time the value of letting go and handing over. Now here I was searching for God and for answers on the Camino, where providence was paramount.

The Spanish phrase *solo y a pie* ("alone and on foot") is closely associated with Ignatius of Loyola as it captures the key movements and journeys of his life. Here, on the Camino, I could relate to Ignatius's state of being in motion, open and trusting, as being tangibly close to God. On the road I had come to understand that God is a pilgrim too, actively searching for me rather than being static, confined, or rigid. I always liked the definition of God as a verb,[101] proactively engaging me in a divine dance,[102] a thrilling and often scary relationship. On the Camino I had been strongly challenged to let go of my burden, to find God in the immediate experience, and to accept real friendship and connection with others. I regularly felt that I was being called out of myself, opened up like a budding flower. I had a spring in my step and felt real joy, an unfamiliar emotion since Donal's death.

Donal had been a great believer in providence, but almost as some kind of safety net that would catch him at the last moment. Like most brothers, we fiercely debated every sort of topic, and none more so than religion. He was a great defender of the poor and outcast, strongly identifying with them. His belief in a God who loves and cares for all people, no matter how downtrodden, was impressive. His care for the well-being of others was absolute. He would often glorify destitution and chaos a bit too much for my liking, as if we had no responsibility at all. I found myself thinking about the manner of his death a lot. Did he believe that God would save him from himself in that last awful act of self-destruction? I wondered what kind of a God he found there in that moment and whether he got the deep peace he was looking for. Nonetheless, I believed that a loving God would understand the desperation of those blackest of moments.

Here in the valley it was the perfect morning: the sun shone hazily through the leafy canopy, and a stream looped forward and backward through a series of bridges on the track. As if to confirm this upbeat turn, I met a delightful Spanish grandfather and granddaughter on a stone bridge over a brook, the grandfather's face lit by a serene smile. They were sauntering along, taking their time and enjoying the day, a model of being present and happy. Their joy was infectious—after exchanging a few words with them, I left feeling lifted by the conversation. The valley opened up into a wide floodplain that was divided into rectangular strips of agricultural farmland alternating corn, spelt, beans, and potatoes. The path was now exposed, and the sun beat down fiercely; I longed for some shade.

About noon I arrived in Salas, the principal town in western Asturias, sweaty and hungry. Known as the "Gateway to the West" for its strategic location in the mountains, Salas's main street was dominated by a medieval tower and the impressive Palacio Valdés. On a sugar low, all I could think about was getting calories and fluids fast. Only then would I appreciate my medieval and Roman surroundings. Just as I was deciding what I would do, I saw a familiar blue and white T-shirt coming up the street. I was overjoyed to see Anuk, my Dutch friend, whom I hadn't seen for days. She was in bad shape, however, totally spent in a stupor of fatigue and defeat. I was shocked at how much weight she had lost—she was pencil thin, gaunt, and worn. I bought her a coffee and was also surprised at how unresponsive she was. Intuiting that she needed support, I reminded her of the huge journey that she had already made from Holland and how close she was to finishing and making it home. To my amazement, on hearing these words she sprung right up out of the chair and back onto the Camino without as much as a good-bye. I let her go, having become accustomed to respecting people's rhythms and privacy.

I bought some food supplies and headed up the steep hill out of town just as the sun was descending on its daily arc. Once more I was alone and on foot. On the edge of town a woman in an apron wished me "Buen Camino" and said "Go in peace," which really struck me, as it was almost biblical.[103] Within minutes I was relieved to be in the shade, walking up a steep stony path that was carved precariously into the side of a ravine. On the right the path fell away into a fast-flowing stream, and above me, bizarrely, a four-lane highway hung suspended in the sky, seemingly from invisible supports. Mercifully, no traffic sounds broke the silence of nature. The heat was steadily building. Only a few minutes into the steep uphill climb I felt a stabbing pain in my left Achilles tendon. As I tried to walk through the pain, my leg started to seize up like a rusty wheel, allowing less and less movement.

Overheated, frustrated, and fed up, I threw a private tantrum: *Why does this keep happening?! That's it, I've had it with this trip. I'm so sick of being injured, I'm finished.* Railing against the unfairness, I impetuously considered pushing on, driven by thoughts of my friends ensconced in a cozy hostel at the top of the hill. I had to force myself to let those distractions go, to focus on the present moment and my immediate predicament. Even though my head was generating many seductive reasons to keep going, my body was telling me a greater truth. Made wiser through my previous Camino experiences of injury, I decided to stop. Gradually, calm returned, and I cooled down.

> When making a decision, consider this question: Are you acting out of freedom or compulsion? Do you feel forced to act, or do you feel drawn naturally to a certain path? Ignatius uses the image of a drop of water hitting a stone (clashing, jarring) or hitting a sponge (an ease, a rightness) to capture the difference.

As usual, no one was around to help. I took some anti-inflammatories and did some self-help—stretching and massage—but it didn't seem to make much difference. Then I tried to sleep it off by taking a siesta at the side of the track, staying close to the wall of the steep ravine. Afterward, I felt somewhat refreshed and gingerly began the steep ascent along the river. Within two minutes the pain ripped through my tendon again. I had to face reality and reluctantly decided to call it a day and return to Salas. I hobbled past the same woman with the apron, and she asked why I was going the wrong way on the Camino. And then, to my joy, I met the eighty-year-old Anton again and his Belgian friend Frederick. I knew them well at this point, and we exchanged some news of our adventures. They shared some water with me as I had run out, and I shared some chocolate with them. Finally, I waved a fond farewell to them as they disappeared up the hill.

Back in town at yet another crossroads, I asked myself, *Where do I get help?* I remembered the advice from Ignatius not to panic but to trust in providence. Some solution would turn up eventually, though it seemed unlikely to me at that particular juncture, a stranger in a strange town. Negativity gnawed at me, planting the suspicion that I was probably finished on this Camino adventure. Then suddenly, I remembered I had seen a physiotherapist's office on the hot march into town, and I got to the office before it closed. To my surprise, the physiotherapist, Davíd Fernandez, took me into his office right away. Even though there were a few other patients around, he acted as if I (a sweaty, limping pilgrim) were the most important person in the world. He had me lie down and massaged both my calves, right into the bone, which was excruciatingly painful. He promised me a full recovery by the next day, which I found hard to believe, as I was in even more pain and could hardly hobble.

He bid me a warm farewell, insisting that I immerse my leg in a cold bath that night. (*Have you seen a hostel with a bath?* I wanted to ask him.) As we talked, I had the impression of a very competent and earnest young man, who was intelligent and aware and slightly out of place in this provincial backwater. I imagined him with plans for a big-city lifestyle, far from Salas. He astounded me by charging only €10 for the one-hour consultation. I presumed that having injured pilgrims turn up at his door was a regular occurrence, but he never gave any hint of this. Once again, the kindness and care of virtual strangers was staggering. However, I was to be even more grateful to him the next day.

Limping past the Castillo de Valdés, a fancy hotel built within a medieval castle, I saw to my amazement that the pilgrim menu del día was advertised. Before I knew it, I had walked in, though I felt a bit out of place in their cool leafy courtyard, surrounded by tables dressed in starched linen. Regardless of my dusty, stained trail wear, I was treated royally. As soon as I tasted the velvety smoothness of the Rioja wine, I knew this was going to be special. The starter was *emberzao*, a kind of a pork black pudding wrapped in cabbage leaves, followed by *fabada*, an Asturian stew made of beans, pork sausage, and bacon. Dessert was my favorite: *arroz con leche y frixuelos*, a crepe with rice pudding. It was probably due to the tough day I had had, but I appreciated every single morsel. I made a fool of myself by lavishing praise on each course to the waitress—I had never enjoyed a meal so much. She must have wondered what poor food I had been eating up to now. Again, I felt it was providence that brought me such a culinary gift when I needed it most.

Fortified by the wine, I got myself a room in the same hotel, justifying it in terms of the bath necessary to treat my leg. Walking into my luxurious room felt overwhelming after grubby hostel living. The colors and velvety fabrics were so dazzling and unfamiliar I hardly dared touch them. In contrast, my few well-worn belongings seemed incongruous in this plush setting. I felt the wonder of a child exploring the room, the view, and the historic parts of the hotel. I did feel somewhat ridiculous later though, shivering in the cold bath, thinking, *This Camino will be the end of me!*

Afterward, feeling refreshed, I rushed out to try to get to Mass in the nearby sixteenth-century collegiate church, but to my dismay the priest was just finishing. I went up to talk to him after, and he introduced himself as Padre Adán, a friendly young man who was pastor for a number of churches nearby. I explained who I was and what I was doing, and to my great joy he said he would be delighted to facilitate my celebrating Mass then and there. He generously offered to be my server, which really touched me. Whether it was the solemn air of the empty church or the novelty of the words in Spanish, I heard them as if for the first time:

*Te damos gracias, Señor y Padre nuestro, te bendecimos y te glorifi-camos, porque has creado todas las cosas y nos has llamado a la vida.*

"We give you thanks, Lord and Father, we bless you and glorify you, because you have created everything and called us into life."

The words spoke to my heart—they felt like a call to life, to rediscover something lost. I was grateful for all I had received on this particularly full day on the Camino. Mostly, however, I was overwhelmed with emotion and choked up on the Eucharist.[104] I don't know what poor Padre Adán thought of this sentimental Irishman, but for me the import and meaning of this day was caught up in the rite, making it difficult to finish this most intimate celebration. To top it all off, Padre Adán went to his car and brought me a bag of pan dulce, which would last me several days. I found all this hospitality a bit too much, this overwhelming generosity of strangers.

Just as the physiotherapist promised, my leg was as good as new the next day. I began again on that long, winding road uphill. Fortified by all the necessary food for the journey and all the support, I arrived in the cold and windy hilltop town of Tineo, some twenty kilometers away, without event.

# 11

# Desolation Road

A sharp sound fractured my unconsciousness, and I awoke with a jolt. Though the hostel was a warm refuge from the mountain air, it had been noisy the night before, with almost every bed taken. Initially there was a lot of rustling and creaking as forty-odd people settled down for the night. At 2 a.m. one couple dragged their mattresses out to sleep beside the toilets, and another pair rose at 5 a.m. to get on the road early. But it was the departure of a large Spanish group accompanied by lots of flashlights, Velcro ripping, and whispered conversations that woke me. I pulled the nylon pillow around my ears but couldn't block it out. Never good in the morning, my nerves were particularly fractious that day. I had a bad feeling about the day ahead.

Bleary-eyed and drained, I forced myself up. Grabbing my backpack, I almost tripped over the couple sleeping beside the toilets. Once outside, the dark slowly dissolved as the sun rose. The path took the same steep trajectory as the sun. Mountains were everywhere, as far as the eye could see—a "terrible beauty"[105] in a crimson dawn. I felt truly insignificant crawling my way westward on this fragile quest. My motivation was dissipating like the mist. I wondered why my spiritual comfort seemed to ebb away at these liminal moments.[106] Turning back to the path, I felt the cold reach of the mist's icy fingers through my light hiking clothes. Although I had put on virtually every stitch I had, the clothes barely warmed me. I regretted not bringing winter woollies—one of the costs of traveling light. The path continued to rise, gradually working its way up onto a wooded shoulder.

Intense greens, russets, and creams—a patchwork quilt of the Asturian farmland—were laid out at my feet. Sparking a memory, my heart ached for home. The land was identical to our family farm, which Donal and I had played on as youngsters and then taken responsibility for when our father died. Once, we had desperately worked to save the harvest after a bad summer. Unfortunately, due to inexperience, we had rushed the process, and the bales turned into a musty, fetid mess. I could almost taste failure again now that my own Camino journey was equally disintegrating through injury and lack of fitness. I was enveloped by hopelessness and despair. Disrupted sleep and a minimal breakfast had considerably reduced my energy reserves, and I hugged myself against the cold. This day would test the depth of my resolve. Like Van Morrison's song, it really was the "Hard Nose the Highway."[107]

The day clouded over and was robbed of any real heat. Despite the early start I was barely able to keep my normal pace—a cumulative effect of wear and tear, but also a new weariness that sapped my spirit. I trudged up to an 820-meter crest called Piedratecha (literally "stone ceiling"), an ominous name given my ever-diminishing abilities. I was overtaken by a Dutch couple who had walked from Irún on the French border as I had. We talked briefly and took a break together on the mountain crest. It was a desolate place, a sandy junction of two trails flanked by stone walls and surrounded by scrub. In contrast to me, the couple seemed in remarkably good shape and eminently confident about an on-time arrival in Santiago. I was beginning to doubt if I would ever escape these endless mountains. From immaculate backpacks they produced flasks of herbal tea and snacks organized in shiny ziplock bags. Seeing my paltry salami sandwiches and water, they offered me hot tea, a real treat. On the descent, I lagged behind them as they strode powerfully ahead. I repeated my well-worn mantra, *Just stick to your own pace.* It was cold comfort, as I could have done with the companionship, especially in this barren place. The eerie swish of windmills on a nearby ridge increased the lonesome feeling.

As they stretched out a lead, what looked like a wild mink suddenly ran out in front of me and headed straight down the path toward the oblivious couple. I called out, but they scarcely had time to turn around before it was gone. A few seconds of precious wildness lifted me. The loping ball of vibrant black fur was a welcome contrast to the dusty farm track. *There are some rewards to trailing behind,* I thought. The rest of the day was still a hard slog though as the trail wound upward through a coniferous forest that turned into a tunnel of interwoven vegetation. Wary of my legs cramping again, I stretched every hour and walked at an ever-slower pace.

I came to a fork in the road high up on a pine-covered hillside, where a sign pointed to a monastery below. The Camino followed the high ground, but I deliberately took the downhill sidetrack to see the Obona monastery, which dated from around the thirteenth century. It was listed as "unmissable" in my guidebook, but I grumbled, knowing I would have to backtrack uphill to this same point. The monastery proved disappointing. Almost in ruins, it was full of ashes and rubble, and badly neglected. The cloister was mostly collapsed, but there was a largely intact nave. I managed to take shelter there during a heavy downpour and have something to eat. This Cistercian monastery had been a huge educational, economic, and agricultural center of power in its day, as well as an important refuge for Camino pilgrims. It was a far cry from that now.

The feeling of being damp, cold, and worn out closed in on me from all sides. I felt like I didn't have much left to give and wondered if I'd be able to finish. Was I just postponing the inevitable by stubbornly refusing to give in? One seductive thought was persistent: *You won't be able to keep doing this for another day, let alone two weeks. . . . No one would blame you if you were to quit.*[108] After all, even the Cistercian monks had given up on this once holy place.

> Sometimes, when we're headed in the right direction guided by God's Spirit, our demons try to drag us down with doubts, obstacles, and worries. The Jesuits tell us to *agere contra*, or act against, and do the exact opposite of what the temptation is.

Having to retrace my steps to pick up the Camino again was dispiriting. The next few kilometers took me through a silent pine forest, a cushion of fragrant needles underfoot. The forest was a temporary relief as I was enclosed in a pine tunnel, a rare comfort in a craggy landscape. Eventually I came to an asphalt road and reluctantly had to put in some "tarmac time," my muscles complaining. In the middle of this penitential stretch, I was cheered when a taxi honked at me and two people waved frantically out the back. It was Frederick and Anton, my two friends from the previous night, who were skipping these difficult stages as they said they would. It hit me what a relief it would be to be transported, not to have to actually walk, to succumb to the comfort. Mostly, I wanted not to have to spend time alone—what I once ironically craved. Painfully aware of the asceticism involved in my pilgrim existence, I longed for mindless diversions and the warm company of friends.

After about thirty minutes of grim slog, I came upon the tiny village of Campiello, high up on a lofty ridge. A ring of rugged peaks dominated the skyline and offered dramatic views in all directions. Though it was still fairly early, I decided to stop here as it was the only albergue for miles and the guidebook darkly hinted at difficult terrain ahead. I collapsed onto a stool in the only place in town, a garish pink-and-white restaurant called Casa Herminia. Crowded already, it had a raucous but friendly feel, like an Irish country bar. Legs of ham and mutton hung by the door, little pools of congealed blood below them. Alongside were assorted farm tools, straw hats, and tourist postcards; a complete grocery store took up another wall. I had some lovely, crusty tuna pie, but I had no appetite and couldn't finish it.

A young German hiker came in, still glowing from the trail, and as there were no free seats, I invited him to sit with me. He spoke excellent English, and we got to talking. I noticed him eyeing my leftover pie and offered him the rest of it, which he readily accepted and devoured. He filled me in on the albergue attached to the restaurant. I gathered that the owner, Doña Herminia, was a materialistic character, charged more (€10), and was not universally liked by hikers. He also told me that the next stage over rock-strewn trails was particularly challenging and had no habitation along the way. It was the infamous "Roof of the Camino" route to El Palo, a brutal climb[109] that sounded menacing. I couldn't shake off a sense of dread that something serious was coming down the line for me. The German decided to go on to the next albergue and take the risk that the small hostel there might already be full. I didn't even consider it, bidding him "Buen Camino." I decided to call it a day and stay where I was. *Play it safe*, I thought, and put off thinking about the next day.

Despite my German friend's caution, Doña Herminia was mentioned positively in my guidebook, which recommended her food and hospitality. I sought her out, this dynamo who ran the albergue and restaurant—and most of the village by the sounds of it. She was lively and engaging, but stress was written in her eyes. She took me on a tour of her "estate," which made up half the village and consisted of a guesthouse of private rooms and a conventional pilgrim hostel, which looked like a converted barn. She was certainly making the most of the Camino boon. I signed in and got my all-important pilgrim stamp. Having had enough of noisy dorms and poor sleep, I opted for one of the private rooms (€27), which were narrow, sparsely furnished prefabs built into the side of the barn.

Once I settled into my room, I went for a walk around the village, a typical farming outpost with agricultural supplies, barns, and a few simple residences on the main street. Sheer drops on the northern side defied any farming attempts. This all added to the isolated, lofty feel of the place, a cold, dramatic mountain aerie. The talk in the albergue below me was all about how to negotiate the difficult next stage. I tried not to think about it. Rather, I went back and tried to distract myself, listening to some music, but nothing worked. Normally, the sounds from nature were all the music I needed, but now I desperately wanted diversion.

A heavy mist shrouded the buildings and farms. With the cold and the wind it transformed this country place into something more sinister. *It might have been a mistake to get a single room and cut myself off so drastically from others,* I thought. At 8 p.m. I made my way across the eerily deserted street to Herminia's restaurant. I had been eating snacks to stave off the gnawing hunger. I could see the clearer outlines of the restaurant now that it was empty. In true Irish style, it was a homely combination of a bar, a grocery shop, and a hardware shop—a one-stop convenience store where you could chat, drink, eat, network, and shop, all from the one bar stool. No doubt this was the locale where everything happened (there was no real competition!). A few barflies were in the corner, and two bartenders were serving, one of whom had Down syndrome and the same ruddy complexion as Doña Herminia. I was the only outsider. It was a bit unnerving to eat alone. Where were all the other hikers?

The food, when it arrived, was wonderful. Herminia served it herself and had probably made it as well. She brought *empanadas* (stuffed pastries, typical of the northwest region of Spain), a stew of beans and meat, cured ham and cheese salad, and red wine and rice pudding (my favorite) to finish. She hovered round like a mother, saying, "You have to eat it all up." It was one of the best hostel meals I got on the Camino. I also got Herminia's undivided attention. She had worked out from my registration that I was a priest, and we had a conversation about young people today, the state of the church, married priests, and so on. Eventually, she turned to personal issues in her life. I could see that there was a lot more to her and realized I had misjudged Herminia, being too ready to believe my German friend's criticisms.

I quickly picked up that she was committed to helping pilgrims and to creating a clean, inviting hostel (I had experienced the exact opposite so far). Amazingly, she did a lot of the day-to-day work herself. She told me about how she served in the shop, cooked the meals, looked after the hostel, and looked after her elderly mother, who had dementia. As she described the contours of her life of service, I could see the weight of anxiety and responsibility outlined on her face. There was no mention of any man in her life—it was a solo operation by the looks of it. I was greatly humbled by her trust in me, by how much she needed to talk, and by the crushing weight of her daily round. I promised to pray for her in Santiago. I got up to leave with a heavy heart; there was so much silent suffering and stoicism in the world. It brought me right back to my own quest and interior pain. I fled, needing some respite.

The loneliness of my little rustic room settled in around me. My heart ached from all that this day had brought—the sense of impending doom, the terrifying trail ahead, my own dwindling energy, and the hopelessness of my task. The obstacles ahead took on gargantuan proportions as I felt my diminished abilities peter out. I would never be able to keep up the pace needed to punch through the Roof of the

Camino. For the first time, I seriously considered quitting. Just thinking about it brought me some relief and a sense of escape from the pain. I texted a close friend of mine that I was thinking of stopping, to test the idea out on him. *This is it*, I thought. *This is where it all comes to an inglorious end.* My Spanish odyssey had reached a real crux, the imposing Asturian mountains had forced me to surrender.

The only thing I dreaded now was doing my night prayer (Review of the Day), as my mind had already congealed around the decision to stop. Tired of it all, I wanted everything to be nice and simple and to have God go along with my decision. I sat down on the bed reluctantly, fighting the impulse to lie down and sleep. As I went back over the day from Tineo to here, I saw all the dark moments

> The Examen (or Review of the Day) is one of the most powerful ways to discover God in our daily life. This five-step prayer helps us see the day through God's eyes:
>
> 1. Ask for God's grace.
> 2. Give thanks.
> 3. Review the day.
> 4. Ask for forgiveness.
> 5. Look forward with God.

clearly: the cold start, the killer hills, the wasted detour to the monastery, the dull pace, the shroud of mist, and the isolation. There had been some "lights"—the mink appearing, talking to Herminia—but they were few, at least so it seemed. I knew that the prayer needs to begin with God's view of the day, but I struggled to find some gratitude.[110] I quickly realized that I had been in a low and pessimistic mood all day. I had essentially picked up on all the notes of discouragement and defeat that I came across. With a jolt, I understood that I was experiencing what Ignatius calls "desolation," a loss of peace and a disturbing unease.[111] This subtle, undermining negativity summed up my entire day. No wonder I was for packing it in!

Immediately I thought of Donal, who had been similarly overrun by negativity in his life.[112] I had seen firsthand the corrosive effects of the depression that ate away at his soul, imposing a cruel black filter on reality. He had struggled to interpret his increasingly bleak thoughts, sometimes being able to get perspective but mostly sliding into an angry, emotional cesspit. I had tried unsuccessfully to be the corrective counterbalance, to point out the kink in the lens, but the negativity was too strong. Still, I felt responsible after his death. I could readily recall all the things I wished I had done differently. The last years I saw him pulled more and more to the "dark side," a world of interior agony that those who loved him could only observe with helpless horror. This was desolation writ large, I realized, my brother internalizing a deceptively negative perspective on life.

I remembered that Ignatius had a series of guidelines about handling desolation, and the key one was not to change a decision that you had previously made in consolation.[113] This is not to say that details can't be changed (as I had done earlier on the Camino), but these key decisions—the crucial supports for our lives—that were made in peace and positivity should not be undone in a low moment. I had an image of me hanging onto a tower while a gale blew. I didn't want to mess with the tower now that I was feeling the force of the wind. I calmed down, and some peace returned. I knew instinctively that I had to hand this whole trip over to God, to something greater than myself, to be able to continue.[114] God was my only support now.

As I began to plan for getting back on the road the next day, my mood and spirits rose. *That was a close call*, I thought. *I almost abandoned the whole thing*. I felt gratitude toward Ignatius for getting me back on track, teaching me to see things through God's eyes. I

> Gratitude is the key to the Examen. As we savor the blessings in our day and realize how much we are loved, we will begin to look at the world in a new way, God's way.

had been given another chance, one of many on this unpredictable trip. On cue, my phone beeped with a reply from my friend, who simply said, "Don't give up." Touched, my eyes welled up and I wept. I rolled into bed and slept well.

# 12

# Saving Sarah

Everything hurt as I awoke to a grey and drizzly day that reflected my mood. I unenthusiastically scraped the disparate pieces of my gear together and closed the door on yet another hostel. I had a quick breakfast in Herminia's bar, greeting her like an old friend. I polished off the eggs and bread quickly. It was strange—although I had only arrived the day before, I felt like I had lived a lifetime in this village. I found leaving difficult, always being the one saying good-bye, always going ahead to the next destination.

Still shaken by the watershed that had been Campiello and how close I came to giving up, I tentatively took to the road again. Deep down I knew that my own resources were threadbare and that this Camino, this quest, was in the hands of God now. It was humbling and painful to confront my own limits, but scarily liberating not to know what was coming next. I repeated the familiar words "Into your hands, O Lord, I commend my spirit,"[115] spoken by Jesus on the cross at the hour of his death. In a strange way the whole experience on the misty mountain had been a "death" for me. I was almost surprised to be alive and on the move again, albeit gingerly, but felt grateful for the small wonders of being healthy, mobile, and relatively intact.

I knew I was going to have to take to the hills again, not something I relished. I grimly read in the guidebook that the next section was the most difficult yet, describing it as a "leg breaker," "not to be done in the rain" and "not to be done alone."[116] I mentally ticked off the boxes in my head: I have breakable bones, it is raining, and I am alone. Once again I found myself weighing the options in Ignatian style. The key was to make a good decision given the reality of my abilities and not be seduced by false motivations. In my life I was tired of pushing myself too hard and paying the price—the Camino was showing me this clearly.

While in Manresa, Spain, from 1522 to 1523, Ignatius himself came to understand that his severe and excessive penances were not healthy (he did some lasting damage) and that he needed to find a more balanced way. Eventually he realized that he was being seduced by the extreme—things that were good in themselves (fasting, penance)—but when taken to the extreme were damaging. Ignatius learned the importance of "indifference": being free of one's own agenda in order to listen to what God is saying. I sought this radical freedom to do God's will.[117]

First, though, I had to identify all my "unfreedoms," or resistances. To begin with, the unwritten Camino rule that you have to "walk all the way" had a certain grip on me. Examining it in the light of my predicament, it seemed unconvincing, as it had already gotten me injured before. In terms of the pilgrimage, the rule was nice to have but not a requirement.[118] It seemed better to assess my present health and fitness and make a decision from there, looking within rather than without. Also, I knew from bitter experience that it was better not to push myself to the extreme[119] right after

> At the beginning of his spiritual journey, St. Ignatius was a man of extremes. He would kneel for seven hours straight, wear prickly clothing, not eat for a week, let his fingernails and toenails grow, cut a hole in his shoes to suffer more while walking—all to enact severe penances. He later realized how much damage he had done to his health, and he learned to be more prudent and balanced.

having had a break or a health crisis. It seemed prudent not to put myself in a situation of risk when I was feeling fragile and not fully fit. For all those reasons I didn't take the high road and instead got a lift to the next town, Pola de Allande. I was to sleep for the rest of the day, which certainly did me no harm.

Pola de Allande is a curious town. I saw it first from the road above as it uncoiled its way into a dense nest of buildings in a narrow river valley. With high-sided hills around, Pola de Allande gave the impression of having been shoehorned into the river Nison's steep ravine. The town dates from the thirteenth century and owed much to the migratory cattle trade that dominated its upper hills. It had "country" written all over it (like most of Asturias), and though this was heartening, there was something dark and dour about the town that was hard to separate from my listless mood. Constant rain and drizzle didn't help. I dodged from sodden veranda to doorway to try to get a sense of the place but eventually gave up. After ruminating in my room for a while, I wanted to get away from this place.

A strong memory came to me of the devastation visited on my family and me in the fallout from Donal's death. There was the numbness and the shock in the immediate aftermath,[120] but I didn't foresee the absolute pit of distress in the years that followed. Long after the rituals and memorial cards were filed away, a desperate wound emerged that defied understanding or healing. The lesion remained open, the nerve ends exposed to a brutal lack of healing or closure. The various areas of my life—work, relationships, health, and prayer—all took a nosedive. The thread and fabric of life, once so rich in meaning, fell away to reveal the ugliness of existence. Life became an agony of moments and a clawing through the days.

The sudden, violent, unannounced exit of Donal from our lives left us all bereft and beaten, wondering what personal failures we had contributed to this catastrophe. As the oldest and as a priest I felt acutely responsible. How had I failed to protect the one closest to me? I lashed out at God: "How could you have let this happen?" "You promised to protect me, to protect him!" "Where were you on that darkest of nights that wrecked our lives so completely?" There were no answers, only an awful silence and the drift into depression that comes with hopelessness.

I came back to my current reality as the evening light faded to grey in the skylight above. Suddenly, I knew I was faced with a sharp dilemma. I was running out of time: I had only ten days left till my flight home and still had more than 220 kilometers to go, with some of the toughest walking ahead of me. I had to face some tough decisions (again). I shared my troubles over coffee with a Spanish couple I had met, Marga and Manolo. Once again, they were Camino regulars, and I had a feeling they were not impressed with me. (I suspected they were tough trekker regulars who were not into my tardy tactics.) They bluntly put my options to me thus:[121]

- Abandon the Camino now.
- Walk on and see how far you get.
- Skip a few stages ahead to ensure you arrive in Santiago de Compostela on time.

I pondered these mutually exclusive options. I reacted strongly against the first option; I had come so far and through so many different crises that I wasn't for quitting now. The second option was intriguing but starkly put. Effectively this is what I had been doing, ambling along and putting off the impact of all my delays. Walking on was appealing but had a false ring to it when I realized I would never actually get to Santiago; I would come up some one hundred kilometers short. It was only in considering the third option that I felt a fire ignite in my belly.[122]

I really wanted to get to Santiago, not because of any trivial need to complete the walk or prove anything, but because I wanted to deliver Donal's T-shirt there. I had promised my brothers and sisters that I would do this, and I intended to deliver on my promise. It was more important to me than reputation or glory or fame. I had drifted a little off course on this quest, but I had clarity again, and incredibly I had a window whereby I could still make it in time.

> To capture the idea about being transformed by God's love, St. Ignatius often used the saying, "Go, set the world on fire." He believed a person is never the same after being touched by the divine. The phrase is a powerful motivator to use our own gifts and talents to shine a light in dark places and ignite sparks, knowing that God will fan the flame.

I thanked the Spanish couple and beat a hasty retreat to my room—I needed to make plans. Shaking off a sense of guilt and shame at "breaking one of the rules," I decided to take public transport the following day to the next city, Lugo. I went down and checked with reception about what transport options were available for the morning and then began the familiar packing routine. I felt charged with a new sense of urgency and optimism—it was like an effervescent current had been introduced into the gloom. I was on a mission again! I would be glad to shake off the murkiness of this town. However, I had learned some important lessons and gained some valuable insights here, and for that I was grateful.

The next morning I was on the footpath with backpack in hand, anxious for the departure. It wasn't going to be easy to get out, as I was still deep in the mountains and there was little transport or infrastructure. The only option was a bus to a nearby town around midmorning, so I had to wait. It was raining as I approached the bus shelter, and the sky was a steel grey. Once again I felt the oppression of the place, hemmed in as we were by steep hills. At the bus stop I met Sarah, a young Dutch hiker, who was apparently having trouble with

her feet. She had bandaged heels, wore open sandals, and had difficulty walking. It turned out that the heavy mountain boots she began
in were shredding her heels and toes. She told me she couldn't put up
with the pain anymore and was going where I was going, Lugo, to
buy new boots.

Like many Camino conversations, we dispensed with the small talk
and got straight to the heart of things. As we got talking she shared
with me that someone had attempted to sexually assault her at the
start of the Camino. I felt for her and sensed that she was close to
quitting, given so many obstacles in her path. I didn't realize it clearly
at the time, but her journey and mine were to become briefly intertwined as we both got through these mountains and out to freedom.
Another Spanish woman who had damaged her knee and had just
been to the doctor that morning joined us at the bus stop. It really
was the confraternity of the "walking wounded," the casualties of the
Camino, and I had to count myself among them.

We took the bus to the village of Grandas de Salime, some forty
kilometers away, and what a ride it was. We initially had to climb a
tortuous grind out of the valley to a lofty sky road. When we weren't
in a whiteout mist at a thousand meters, we were racing along knife-
edged ridges and taking stomach-churning hairpin bends. Apart from
the white-knuckle ride, the journey managed to reveal some of the
most beautiful mountain country, with a *Lord of the Rings* quality.
Forested ridges, alpine meadows, and isolated homesteads stretched
off as far as the eye could see. Getting into town was a relief, though,
as I was fairly green at that stage, needing some time to recover over
a cola.

Soon, Sarah was urging me on, keen to get to civilization quickly
and to get her feet sorted out. I realized at this stage that we were a
team and that my mission, as she didn't speak Spanish, was to be her
translator and guide to get her where she needed to go. The problem

was that we were in yet another little highland town without onward bus connections. We needed to get across to another mountain town, A Fonsagrada (meaning "sacred fountain," whose origin is attributed to St. James the apostle), to make the vital bus connection to Lugo.

Charged up, I went into the first shop that was open on the main street, an old-style bookshop, where I met the two nicest women. They told me that the only means of getting to A Fonsagrada was by taxi and, coincidentally, the husband of one of the women was a taxi driver. I was getting on so well with them that Sarah had to come in and get me. Within a few minutes, the taxi pulled up, and we piled in our hiking gear. I was beginning to enjoy this new adventure and my new traveling companion. Things were working out better than I had hoped.

The journey took only twenty minutes, again at an altitude of one thousand meters (i.e., about 3,200 feet), but it was done at high speed and with uncompromising cornering. I felt like we were crossing some great forbidding desert, escaping terrible badlands or fleeing from desperate foes. The dramatic geology, the remoteness, and the barren uplands seemed to mirror the difficult experiences we had both been through in the previous days. I understood the importance of changing the environment as a symbol for inner movement and openness to new possibilities.

The exhilarating taxi ride delivered us to A Fonsagrada, where we would get the all-important bus to our destination, Lugo. The only problem was that the departure was not for four hours—all that speed for nothing. One thing the Camino teaches is the art of wasting lots of time in public places, and so we walked until we found a park with some benches shaded by oak trees. We shared our simple pilgrim fare, some fruit, bread, olives, and cheese. The conversation ranged from our experiences on the Camino, which were always diverse, to the inevitable medical ailments that plagued us. It was particularly painful to watch Sarah hobble around on her lacerated feet, which I hadn't really noticed until now.

The conversation took a deeper turn when Sarah took out a prayer book and told me what she did for a living.[123] I learned that my new pilgrim friend was actually an Anglican minister and a theologian. Imagine my surprise and then hers as I filled her in on my being a Jesuit priest and school chaplain. There was something apt and ironic about this situation, being travelers from very different backgrounds on the same road who are thrown together in this way. We passed the time enjoyably, tackling different theological and ecumenical points, but it was on the topic of prayer that we found agreement. Eventually we settled ourselves to read the office from her *Book of Daily Prayer*. I found it surprisingly like the Divine Office I was used to. We passed the book back and forth reading psalms and epistles. At one stage I was amazed to see her produce a Bible as she sought out a Gospel text. The text was one well known to me:

> Blessed are those who mourn, for they will be comforted. Blessed are those who hunger and thirst for righteousness, for they will be filled. Blessed are the merciful, for they will receive mercy. Blessed are the pure in heart, for they will see God.[124]

Read in that context alongside my crippled companion, the words took on an increased meaning and import. I could keenly identify with my twofold mission, both as the grieving brother and now as the humble helper.[125] I saw a tear escape from under Sarah's sunglasses and knew the words had hit home for her, too.

Eventually the long-awaited bus arrived, and we took our seats for the third leg of that momentous day. This was to be a testing journey, getting baked by the evening sun on a stiflingly hot minibus, with little or no views. At one stage I was excited to see my friends Frederick and Anton sitting at a roadside bar. I waved frantically at them, but they seemed to be dazzled by the sun and disappointingly didn't react. The countryside became more pedestrian and less stark as we came down from the high mountains toward Lugo. We had escaped the mountains and whatever paralysis they had exerted on us. To celebrate our escape, we had a pilgrim meal and a glass of wine together in the twilit main square. Then we went our separate ways, as I was walking the next day and she was buying new boots. Part of the pain of the Camino is the intensity of encounters followed by the separation as journeys diverge. That night, doing my Review of the Day, I felt that God had been very close to me all day. I had made the right decision to jump ahead in the Camino, and meeting Sarah was a real bonus. Whatever help I might have given to her, I felt I had received much more. It had awakened something in me that I long feared had been extinguished. Specifically, accompanying Sarah had restored my sense of compassion and care for others, something that suicide grieving had robbed me of.

# 13

# Deliverance

I opened my weary eyes and wondered where I was. The hotel ceiling and narrow little room swam into focus, and eventually I remembered the previous day's bus journey to Lugo with Sarah. As my body creaked out of bed, I thought, *My last week*, with some excitement. I really wanted to finish quickly at this stage, and one hundred kilometers sounded doable in four fast days. Little did I know what was ahead of me. . . .

All my gear looked a bit rough, and I did too. I decided not to look in mirrors anymore. I got a quick coffee and croissant in the cafeteria downstairs and was on the road by 7:30 a.m. A thick mist and dull, flat light made the Roman walls and gates even more imposing. The bitter cold hurried me along to get warm. Initially I had trouble finding the Camino markers—the scallop shells—set into the pavement. Eventually I caught up with two tall Spanish hikers who had this slow, relaxed lope that was deceivingly efficient, as I was to find out. They directed me ahead through the city walls, but in my haste I forgot their directions and ended up following a circuitous route that brought me out behind them once more. *More haste, less speed*, I thought.

Somehow, I had lost my own relaxed rhythm and was back in race mode, some of it brought on by "finishing fever," but also by a certain amount of exhaustion that clouded my judgment. On the way out of town I passed three Spanish women who would shortly overtake me as I stopped to do my stretches by the broad river Miño. I felt a worrying jagged pain in my left calf muscle, and no amount of stretching seemed to ease it. I bitterly regretted going too fast earlier, but I had to let go of this now. Ignatius would have counseled me to be free and detach from this corrosive emotion in order to deal well with the present. I looked up to my right to see a twenty-meter-wide floating bridge that had been constructed across the river. Curiously, it was fitted with ladders, seats, and decking, effectively turning the whole river into a swimming pool. It looked a bit crazy to me; normally I would have inspected it closely, but I was more interested in walking again.

I had hoped for an easy saunter toward Santiago, but now I faced a battle to see how far my leg would take me. I had hoped for a wooded track but instead was subjected to a tarmac surface and a quiet back road. I had also hoped for a little café along the way, but there was none. All these hopes were killing me now as I struggled to let go. Thankfully I fell into step with one of the Spanish women I had passed earlier. I was grateful for the company and for how the distance shortened with the chat. She and her two friends had just started that day (Monday) and were looking to get to Santiago by Wednesday. I admired such optimism and certainty. One of them set herself up as the leader, striding ahead at a brutal pace. I reflected on how often I had done this, trying to force reluctant pilgrims up mountains in Ireland. I could see the folly of it now and the lack of tolerance and compassion it espoused. I resolved to do things differently when I got back. Eventually I had to let the women go, slowed by pain as I was, and was gradually overtaken by all the others.

With no pilgrims and no traffic, the little Galician country road suddenly became terribly lonesome. I could feel that familiar dreaded muscular spasm in my calf, a crippling stabbing pain that rippled out as the muscle contracted. I tried to ignore it for a while and keep up a moderate but hobbling pace. It only worsened, so I stopped to do some more stretching, rub on some anti-inflammatory cream, and massage it. Nothing worked. A certain tide of panic rose as well as deep frustration and resentment—it was so unfair. I gasped for air, struggling to let those feelings subside.

Unable to walk, I cast off my rucksack. *This is it. This is where it all ends. The Camino is over for me; now I'll have to go home.* The bitter thought was laced with some relief and resignation as I conceded, *I just want the pain to stop.* Another part of me was outraged with the constant injuries and enforced stops that got in the way of progress. I had to force myself to go into a deeper place, away from the morass of anger, blame, escapism, and avoidance. Thinking of Ignatius sick and wounded gave me some distance to get perspective on what I was doing. I formed a little prayer: "Over to you, Lord. I am totally out of options here."

Feeling a bit more centered, I thought to myself, *Hold on. Before giving up totally, let's look at the options here. What can I actually do?* I gazed around for inspiration. I thought I might get a lift, but there was no traffic, only trees. Alone and isolated, I realized I was going to have to get myself out of this. What to do? I reckoned that I could, ignoring the pain, probably hobble on for another two to three kilometers maximum. It was too far to go back to Lugo. If I didn't find help soon—I'd be in real trouble. Still, God hadn't let me down so far. I got up and, gritting my teeth and using my pole as a crutch, began a lame shuffle at a snail's pace. Then it began to rain, and I kept focused as best I could, trying to dispel the despairing thoughts. It was the longest walk on what had been a hard road so far.

I thought of Donal, when he had had a breakdown. I was helping him on the farm and had also arranged some medical appointments for him, one of which was with a specialist in Derry, some two hours away. We set off in our old diesel car, and running late as usual, I overtook a number of cars on a rare straight stretch (with Donal egging me on, I might add). Then, to my horror, an oncoming SUV appeared, heading straight for me, and I couldn't get back into the line of cars. If the SUV driver hadn't swerved off the road and driven onto the shoulder, it would have been a head-on collision. I pulled off on the same shoulder and came to a stop in shock, my fingers buried in the steering wheel like a cartoon character. Donal got out to deflect the wrath of the SUV driver, who was irately bearing down on us. Here was Donal batting for me when I was supposed to be looking after him. Strangely, I felt the same now, that my brother was protecting me, that disaster had been averted, and that good could come out of this situation. It gave me strength.

Just when I thought I would pass out or fall to the ground, I came to the tiniest of villages. O Burgo comprised about four farmhouses clustered around a crossroads. I knew I couldn't expect a doctor or a pharmacy way out here, but to my enormous relief there was a sign for a bar just down a side road. Grimacing, I limped down the long gravel drive and gasped out my order, "Café con leche, por favor." When I finally shook my attention from my own pain, I was initially repelled by the place. There were legs of smoked ham hanging in the rafters above a beer-stained bar counter, and timbers browned with years of smoke. Flies buzzed around me, and an old lady with an intimidating demeanor limped in to attend the bar. I almost panicked. I was stranded here, off the Camino, in an empty bar in a very vulnerable position, and unable to walk. I was wary, unsure as to whether I could trust her, yet forced by circumstances to be there.

Just for a moment I had a flashback to the U.S. backwoods movie *Deliverance*, where local inbred Georgia natives attack a group of middle-aged canoers. What starts out as a fun outdoor adventure dramatically turns into a nightmare struggle for survival. I thought maybe I had stumbled on some unredeemed corner of Galician wilderness. For a moment I saw myself skewered, smoked, and salted in the rafters. I shrugged off the image, forcing myself to focus on the present. I put words together for a brief conversation, seeing the bar lady as more benign and human now. I realized the negative effects of the inhuman, agonizing walk I had just been on. I remembered one of Ignatius's rules for deciding well: "Don't make hasty decisions when you're low, but also be proactive against the negativity,"[126] so I put my imaginings to the side and gratefully tucked into my milky coffee and biscuits. As my blood sugar levels rose, I started to feel substantially better.

Feeling my humanity returning, I struck up a conversation with the bar woman, whose name was Consuelo.[127] She turned out to be very pleasant, and I quickly got down to the key questions. Did they have any rooms? She said they had a bunk in a lean-to on the roof of the pub. Did they offer food? She said she could give me lunch and dinner for a reasonable price. I couldn't believe my luck. *Thank you, God*, I whispered to myself. Warming to the situation, I asked the key question: did she have some painkillers? She kindly offered me her own prescription medicine for her bad hip—she was generosity herself! I downed one of the packets mixed with water, seeking some relief from my throbbing leg ache.

Before long I realized that her medicine was about six times stronger than normal, but I wasn't feeling any pain, and that was the first time that day. I marveled at how the day had turned around from the edge of disaster, how I had everything I needed in this rustic pub, and how my own emotions and preconceptions had been the biggest barriers. It was a radical lesson in trusting in providence, in goodness, even in the most unlikely setting. It was 10 a.m., and the most eventful part of the day was over. All was right with the world.

I took my second coffee outside to some chunky garden seats that I guessed had been made in the woodshop next door (dismissing any *Texas Chainsaw Massacre* images). A soulful-eyed mongrel lay at my feet, the sun warmed my back, and I felt blissful. The silence was broken by the arrival of a group of four Belgian undergrad students who were looking for beer. Once they had placed their order, we introduced ourselves, and inevitably the talk turned to the Camino. They were on their first day and wanted to walk the last 100 kilometers as the minimum to get the official certificate, the Compostela. With the optimism of youth they were determined to reach Santiago in three days, which was pretty ambitious. When I questioned this, one responded flatly, "We have to get there." As I looked at their flip-flops, their big rucksacks, and the cans of beer strapped on top, I certainly wished them all the best and prayed for them.

Consuelo, meanwhile, couldn't have been more pleasant and helpful, completely dispelling my initial impression. She brought me upstairs to my bunk, which was in a bizarre annex on the roof of the pub. It was a familiar hostel-type room with two bunks, but I would have the room to myself. I could hardly believe my luck. After a delightfully long and pain-free siesta I came down for the trusty menu del día prepared by Consuelo. I was ravenously hungry after the day I had had. She brought out a mixed tuna salad with lots of olives to start, followed by a tender cut of veal with fries and greens, and ending with a simple bowl of ice cream—which was a step up from the normal tub of yogurt. Desserts had been a bit poor on the Camino, but at €10 for everything, including a glass of wine, I wasn't complaining. One of the great pleasures of the Camino is being grateful for your food, the fruits of hard walking, and a heightened awareness of the wonderful activity of eating.

A large man dressed in heavy work clothes was eating at another table, and by following the conversation I deduced that he was

Donal (bottom) and I (top) on holiday in Donegal

Donal at a family gathering on the farm

Outside San Sebastian on the third day of the Camino

Confusing signpost in the Basque Country

Alone and on foot in the early morning in Basque Country

The wine region outside Deba near the coast

Hiking the seaside route with my German friend Willy

Santa Juliana procession in Santillana del Mar

The festival procession at Comillas with the parish priest (left) and
Miguel (middle)

Back on the Camino again at Oviedo with my new insoles

Bridge over the river Nalón near Grado

A sixteenth-century collegiate church window in Salas, Asturias

Eighty-year-old Anton (left), Frederick (right), and I outside Tineo

The Cantabrian Mountains, also known as the infamous "Roof of the Camino"—and my biggest challenge—surround the town of Pola de Allande.

The ever-upbeat Alvarez family outside Melide

On arriving in Santiago de Compostela Cathedral

The place of "the burning" in Cape Finisterre

Feeling the joy of release moments after the burning

Consuelo's husband, Jaime. He ran the huge carpentry workshop next to the pub. Again, if I were to go on his appearances (scruffy, dour, withdrawn), he was an axe murderer, but fortunately I had already learned that lesson. We got on great, and he took me on a tour of the workshop. Then the two of us became engrossed in a dubbed Sean Connery film, *Outland*, which was showing on the television in the corner. It was a surreal space western but provided some much-needed escapism. After the film, Jaime took himself outside and lay down on a bench, where he was soon fast asleep.

Feeling considerably better, I asked Consuelo what there was to see around here—the village itself was a huddle of houses barely one hundred meters long. She directed me to an old church in the woods nearby. It took me a long time to find it, but the country lane leading there was the epitome of tranquillity, and I was lost in gratitude for the wonder of creation, being alive, and being able to walk gingerly.

I had walked past it before I realized it: unsigned and practically invisible, the old church was set back from the road. It was beautiful in its simplicity, probably built in the seventeenth or eighteenth century, almost completely constructed of stone with a few timbers. The glen's atmosphere of peace and calm was such that I speculated that the chapel was once on the Camino. It certainly lulled me into reflection, and I came back to myself feeling rooted and centered after a chaotic morning. I made my way back to the pub again and still had five hours of daylight. I began to read *The Count of Monte Cristo* on my phone in a little chair on the pub rooftop. It was a long but serene evening.

That night I did my Examen as usual in my bunk. Even though it had been a day of crisis and near disaster, everything had turned around once I made that simple decision to keep going on the road. I was filled with gratitude for not only the gift of breaking an old habit of being panicked into poor decisions, but also for the wisdom of St. Ignatius's method of reflection. I felt that something really important had happened, and I was filled with a warm gratitude that permeated my disposition and attitudes toward that day. It was like I was discovering the Examen prayer anew. Like the famous Jesuit leader Pedro Arrupe, I understood the words "More than ever I find myself in the hands of God."[128] If I hadn't before, I believed now that the Camino was out of my hands; it wasn't my project anymore. I was handing it over and was very comfortable with that.

After suffering a stroke, Pedro Arrupe, SJ, wrote this prayer:

*More than ever I find myself in the hands of God. This is what I have wanted all my life from my youth.*

*But now there is a difference; The initiative is entirely with God.*

*It is indeed a profound spiritual experience To know and feel myself so totally in God's hands.*

—Excerpted from *Hearts on Fire: Praying with Jesuits*

The next morning I woke up around seven to the splash of cascading water. I was confused initially, trying to remember where I was (on top of the pub in a flimsy annex, I soon remembered). I thought it was someone showering nearby, but when I got up to peer out the window, I realized it was a deluge of rain hopping off the tarred roof. Since there was nothing I could do, I sank into the soft duvet and went back to sleep. I eventually got up at eight thirty and went down for breakfast at the bar, which was full of drenched pilgrims. Having hardly seen a soul there the day before, it was strange to see so many together, forced in by the rain. I was the only one in dry gear, everyone else was soaked. Amazingly, my leg felt good again—all that rest, painkillers, and diversion seemed to do the trick.

Having had a café con leche and some amazing chocolate croissants (one of the Camino's little pleasures), I bid Consuelo a warm and grateful good-bye. I had learned a lot in this unlikely place about trust and how to let go of judgments; it had been a real deliverance for me. Back on the Camino, I set off, slowly this time, thinking maybe I would manage a realistic ten kilometers that day.

As I looked back on this little insignificant hamlet, I realized that I had been transformed more here than anywhere else. The defining moment of my calf injury and being stranded on the road had forced me to let go and let God operate. Great things certainly came out of it—exactly what I needed in fact. Then there was the overcoming of my fears and stereotypical judgments about Consuelo and her husband. And yet they couldn't have

> Ignatius believed that the worst sin was ingratitude. If we could fully understand all the blessings and love God has given us, we wouldn't act out of fear or selfishness. To combat ingratitude, Ignatius calls us to name and *savor* what we're grateful for—in my case, everything from chocolate croissants to Consuelo's hospitality. In this way, we live in God's love and act differently.

been more caring, generous, and accommodating—they provided for all my needs. I noticed that my initial negative reaction to them as different, a writing them off without knowing them, came out of fear and prejudice. I had so much to be thankful for. St. Ignatius used to say that the lack of gratitude was the only real sin.[129] I knew the truth of this out on the Galician Camino. I consciously remembered what this humble family had done to get me back on the road. I resolved to be a more grateful person, to acknowledge all that I have received, and to live in the glow of gratitude as Ignatius recommends in the Examen prayer.

# 14

# Carried by Kindness

I was getting pretty tired of it all at this stage, so it was really hard to drag myself out of my hostel bunk in the morning. It hadn't helped that I had felt cold during the night—the hostel had only one blanket for me, and I rued leaving my sleeping bag behind to keep the weight down. Then the early risers had departed as subtly as a herd of elephants in hobnail boots. As I was organizing my, by now, distinctly grubby gear, a guy leaned down from a nearby bunk and asked what sounded like "How's your food?"

*My food*, I thought, looking at my plastic bag of groceries. *Have we mice too?* Then I realized that he, a Portuguese man, was asking me about my foot and that I had met him ten days ago on the Camino. He and his girlfriend, the most Irish-looking redhead, invited me to have breakfast with them. I was mighty glad, as I was low on food and sorely needed some companionship to help me get going. Sharing breakfast was never so much about human warmth and so little about food, although the calories helped too. I gave thanks for their humble hospitality.

Reluctantly I took my leave and headed up the mist-covered mountain to a pass through wind turbines. There was something distinctly *Lord of the Rings* about the tenebrous granite path and epic quest that I was on.[130] It was bitterly cold in the beginning, but I soon warmed up with exercise and the mist clearing. The high pass opened out to a wooded valley, and I descended into a green-and-brown patchwork of rushy fields, pines, and moorland. I was grateful there were no more ascents—I was more than done in and stumbling along on autopilot.

Something about this Galician area did not look like Spain though. Suddenly it hit me—it was exactly like a bog road near home in Northern Ireland. I felt like I was home and close to those I loved with these familiar landmarks. I thought of the farm and my family, especially Donal. These were the same roads and fields that we had walked as children out chasing cattle. We were shaped by that landscape, formed from that peaty soil, sculpted by those elements. Finding it recreated in western Spain bolstered me at this difficult moment.

As usual, I was walking alone for several hours. I then caught up with a family I had seen in the hostel the night before. I noticed that two of the teenagers were limping and carrying old nylon frameless packs, which pulled heavily on their backs. I got talking with the aunt, Mariana, and she explained that they were the Alvarez family from Mexico on a European trip. They were four cousins, all teenagers, and she was the only adult. I was impressed by them right away; they were so open and happy, unspoilt by cynicism. I got to know them as we walked along, and the kilometers flew. The pain in my feet increased, and I stopped for a break, thinking I would return to my own company again. They made to go on, but then the aunt asked me to give them a blessing, knowing I was a priest. They all lined up, heads bowed on this dusty broken path on the Spanish Camino. I was humbled and moved so that I was barely able to utter an improvised Spanish blessing. *This is one of those Camino moments for sure*, I thought.[131]

I walked on my own for a bit and then came upon another Portuguese group in a bar who had also been in the hostel. They were in high spirits, anticipating finishing soon, and were having a few beers (even though it was only 10:30 a.m.). I joined in on the fun and felt the better for it, leaving them an hour later. I walked on again, now in increasing heat and back on the asphalt. I caught up with the Alvarez family again, who were going very slowly (they said I was going fast!). I tried to help them adjust their backpacks, which still weighed heavily on their shoulders. We walked the last few kilometers into Melide together, our destination for the day. Melide is actually the meeting point of our Camino, the Primitivo, and the main artery, the Camino Francés. Part of me was sad to leave the mountains and the solitude, for now we would be walking with hundreds on the final approach to Santiago, just over fifty kilometers away. It was so close I could hardly breathe, a combination of excitement, emotion, and exhaustion.

Afterward I went to the parish Mass, where the priest kindly let me concelebrate. I was delighted to see the Alvarez family there and blessed them again at the end of Mass, during the pilgrims' blessing. We had a great reunion in the square after Mass, as if we had all known one another our whole lives. The town was full of hikers from all over, and every other one was either limping, had on a support bandage, or smelled of menthol muscle rub. Many people had blue kinesiology tape on their leg muscles, which gave a new respectability to pulls and strain. As we neared our sacred destination, the extent of the sacrifices involved was visibly evident. That evening I bumped into a Belgian guy, Mikael, whom I had met two weeks earlier when he was setting out from Oviedo with his dad. Suffering from severe tendonitis, he had been told by a doctor to stop walking. So here he was, waiting for his father to arrive, trying to fill the time, abstractly watching cycling on television. He was tuned out and disheartened. It was hard to watch, and even harder to try to console him.

The next morning, I was on the Camino Francés at seven and was a bit put out to see so many people walking already. In fact, from here on I would be saying good-bye to the solitude that I had experienced on the other routes. The morning was overcast and mercifully cool, perfect for walking. I saw all types of people and gear, yet disconcertingly recognized no one. However, around 10 a.m. I came upon the Alvarez family, who were having a snack in the woods. *This is happening a lot*, I thought, but I was happy to join them and share their yogurt and biscuits. I walked with them for a while, now feeling like part of the family. Then I had the mad idea that I would race the youngest boy, Juan Pablo, up the steep incline (they were ribbing me as to who was the fastest walker). He went straight into the lead, and I tried to catch him. I started to run and so did he, and, of course, he beat me to the top, though I pretended I had won. It was great fun—a bit mad in the context, as it took all my residual energy—but it brought us all together.

I reflected that there was something touchingly pure and innocent about this Mexican family. They reminded me of my time in Colombia as a Jesuit student and of the real down-to-earth goodness of the Latin Americans, so compassionate, warm, and transparent. There was something else too though—they reminded me of Donal before depression and mental illness got their talons into him. He had been such a bright light: smart and entertaining, warm and funny, compassionate and prayerful. Then, inevitably, they reminded me of myself before suicide wreaked its devastation, how I had been similarly open and optimistic, trusting and believing. Had I just been naive about the world? Could I believe in hope again? Was there rescue after trauma? Would negativity be overcome? It hurt to think of these things.

Back on the dusty Camino de Santiago, I watched these Mexicans and marveled. They were great fun to be with and strongly encouraged me to walk with them as we neared our goal. I was torn, especially as I felt protective of them, but I was also impatient to get

finished. Saying an emotional good-bye, I walked on. After all, I had
set out on this walk solo, and I didn't want to be picking up passen-
gers so close to the finish. I reminded myself that this was for the best
and pushed on, free and walking fast again. A little voice questioned
whether I had done the right thing, but I ignored it.[132]

An hour later, I had a leisurely but lonely lunch in Arzúa, the main
town. I was pushing hard now, the end almost in sight, and I abandoned my slow pace just to get finished, to get the pain over with. I
was between hostels and knew I would have to do a mammoth fifteen
to twenty kilometers to finish in Santiago the next day. I had to pinch
myself: Santiago? Finishing? After all this time, suffering, and amazing
grace, it would be over. I headed out on the road in the noonday sun,
trusting that something would come up along the way. After about
six kilometers I was beginning to wilt and stopped at a roadside café
for ice cream. I got the impression that it was newly built and specifically for walkers, part of the commercial boon that was the Camino.
It was here that I met the indomitable Portuguese group again, and
I was mightily glad of their company. "Another five kilometers" said
the woman in the café. It seemed like an eternity. About an hour later
I came across a sign for a private hostel that was not on the map, a
godsend.

*Am I in paradise?* I thought as I walked through the gates of Pou-
sada de Salceda, an independent hostel on the Camino. There was a
fountain in the center, a state-of-the art restaurant and bar, and pilgrims sunbathing in the gardens. I was wasted, footsore, and weary
and needed refuge. I treated myself to a room that, though basic,
seemed the ultimate luxury to me. Doing my laundry in the sink was
a delight for once, as the fountain tinkled outside. I had a celebra-
tory beer at the bar, the breeze taking the edge off the Galician sun,
and a lovely dinner alone at a table in the restaurant. That evening,
as the sun was setting, I took myself up a nearby hill where I could

witness the magnificence of this sunset. Brown, gold, and orange tones emanated from the sun, which was setting virtually directly over Santiago, only twenty-eight kilometers away. I wanted so badly to end this odyssey, or survival story, or whatever it had become. But a part of me also dreaded finishing. I didn't want to leave this simple life behind, where I felt so close to God and where things made sense, even amid the unpredictability. I stayed until there was only a silver rim on the horizon, a visual echo of what once was.

I was moved to think of the last time I had seen Donal alive. It was at the beginning of the summer, and he seemed in uncommonly good form. He had moved back into our family farmhouse, living there alone, among the ghosts. Not accustomed to his upbeat mood, I put it down to some kind of recovery (in fact, later I learned that this is one of the danger signs; the person has made a plan and intends to execute it, alleviating their normal distress and anxiety). Like many others, I became an expert in suicide only when it was too late.[133] We spent some time together, and it wasn't long before I realized that this was not the brother I knew.

> My hard-won insights for coping with suicide:
>
> - The goal is to move from being a victim to being a survivor; suicide will always be a part of you.
> - There is often a need for professional suicide/ grief-related help.
> - The most difficult thing is trying to understand why.
> - The suicidal person almost always gives clear clues before the event.
> - The support of family and friends is critical in the recovery process.
>
> —Adapted from Brendan McManus, SJ, "Surviving Suicide," *The Furrow* 61, no. 2 (February 2010)

Fundamentally there was no connection, nothing of the close relationship we had had. We would normally tell each other everything, especially about what was going on inside, how we felt. I was disconcerted to think that my brother was slipping away from me, becoming unreachable, but the outer bonhomie seemed to belie that, and I chose to believe the latter—that he was recovering. Later, this was a source of great pain, guilt, and remorse. Why did I not recognize the signs? Why did I go away on holidays? Why didn't I stay around? The bitter aftertaste lingered.

Back on the Camino, the day started off well. I was up early, and the hostel served breakfast at 7 a.m. (a rarity in itself). The azure sky lifted my spirit. I knew I could make it to Santiago in one day if I really pushed it. What could possibly go wrong? While packing my gear after breakfast, however, I began to experience a strange unease. It was a peculiar feeling, especially when contrasted with the inner anticipation of finishing the Camino. I had to sit back and consciously examine what was happening and fight against my head saying, *Just ignore all that and push on—quick, quick, you're losing time.* It was a familiar battle to me at this stage, forcing myself to slow down enough to be able to listen to what was really going on inside. Ignatius would have been familiar with this when he was convalescing as he was forced by circumstances to listen to the inner voices and discern what was genuinely life-giving and from God.

I knew two things: one was the enormous pressure and excitement of finishing this thing after four weeks on the road and many adventures. I just wanted it to be over and to finally rest, to take off the rucksack and not have to think anymore. The other was this strange, empty feeling, that I was missing something and needed to pay attention to it. I didn't really want to hear this latter voice at this stage—it wasn't where I was at. However, there was something insistent and wholesomely true about it, something I had learned not to ignore.

After some time sitting on my bed and wrestling with it, watching the other hikers leaving, it finally came to me: *It's the Mexican family. They have been inviting you multiple times to join them, and you have refused them. Now is literally your last chance to take up that offer.* I didn't quite understand why God was asking me to take up this paradoxical offer, as they seemed fine on their own. I just knew that this was something I had to do. Ignatius would have called my jarring unease desola-

> Symptoms of desolation:
> - Superficial delight
> - Restlessness
> - Unease
> - Sadness
> - Slothfulness
> - Hopelessness
> - Spiritual dryness; "there is no God"
> - Negativity
> - Drained of energy
> - Feeling cut off or alone
>
> —Excerpted from Margaret Silf's *Inner Compass*

tion,[134] the experience of being out of tune with the Spirit and being pestered by God to get with the program. I delayed my departure by some hours to let the Alvarez family catch up and then set out on the road to find them.

I ambled along the tree-lined path, not pushing it, having learned some hard lessons in that department. I began to get back into the rhythm, like slipping into a well-worn gear. I frequently felt the twinge of some muscle or tendon, so I had to stop to massage the area or stretch. Something was different this morning though: first, I felt completely out of energy, like there was nothing left in the tank, and second, I felt a new sharp pain in the tendon near my left knee. Rather than complain about it, I readily fell into the "injury routine," seeking some medical help and finding a place to rest. I slowly wound my way up the hill into a small town called O Pedrouzo. I had walked only six kilometers, and I was finished. Philosophically I thought, *At this rate I'll be crawling on my hands and knees into Santiago.*

Getting this close to Santiago, I was now seeing the worst of commercialization. For example, people would appear in the middle of nowhere handing out leaflets for their particular hostel or pensión. At one point I was crossing a road and a recorded voice bid me welcome on behalf of some hostel in Santiago—I nearly jumped out of my skin. Now there was a huge variety of public and private accommodation in all the towns and villages on the Camino Francés. Everything was developed around the needs of the passing pilgrim, a far cry from the low-key approach I had experienced earlier in the Basque Country.

As I passed the municipal hostel in town, I was thrilled to see two members of the Mexican family; I had almost given up hope of meeting them again. The teens were first in a queue for the hostel because they had gotten a lift there that morning after hurting their legs and being unable to walk. They were waiting for their aunt and the other two cousins. I decided I would keep them company till the others arrived, as they didn't know how long they'd be. It was a long afternoon, hot and dusty, but we made the best of it. We played some games, speculated on where the others were, and talked. At one point I went off to the pharmacist, where I got a knee support bandage and the very familiar advice: rest, ice, massage, and take anti-inflammatories. Rejoining the teenagers back at the hostel, I joked that the support bandages were infectious, as all three of us were wearing them now. It was getting late in the afternoon, and I realized they hadn't eaten, so I made them some sandwiches from my hiking supply. This simple meal of breaking bread and sharing water moved me to reflect on the Mass and on how the life-giving flesh and blood of Christ was a supreme act of love for us. It was the giving of his very self, the ultimate selflessness that I had witnessed many times on the Camino.

They asked how I came to be a priest—they were Catholic and intensely interested—not something I was used to at home. At this stage they were getting worried about the others as they were long overdue. We tried to work out what we could do to contact them. Just as we were beginning to despair, the three walkers arrived in great form. Following a happy reunion, the group decided to stay in a pensión, and I got a room above theirs. That evening, we all went to Mass together at the local church, firm friends at this stage. The only problem I had was beginning Mass with the other celebrants; they genuflected at the altar, but I only made it halfway down due to the agonizing pain in my knee. I was struck by the lovely blessing for pilgrims they had at the end of Mass, and I got to bless the Alvarez family again.

The next morning, I woke at six and threw open my room's windows. *This is going to be it—it has to be,* I thought and, moved to tears, watched the sun struggle to rise from behind a wall of clouds. Finishing the Camino would be the end of my struggle. I prayed for a while, handing it all over to God, the suicide and the pain, and asked for help with the day to come.[135] I had arranged to meet the Alvarez family at 7 a.m. so we could walk together. One of the injured girls, Milli, was getting the bus and would meet us later, while one of the boys, José Carlos, had made a miraculous recovery. We set off at a nice pace and were surprised that there were so few hikers on the road. Having had no breakfast, I had to stop for coffee after an hour to get energy. They were good enough to wait for me even though I told them to go on. About then I realized that they were carrying me; I was completely done in.

That was one of the most painful days of walking in my life. I don't know whether it was the buildup of lactic acid, accumulated injuries, or prolonged effects of dehydration, but this day sapped all my remaining resources and will. I felt like I was stumbling along on two stumps for feet, and although they were numb from repeatedly hitting the ground, the pain was always there. I had a bitter, acidic taste in my mouth that nothing could wash away.[136] It was all I could do to keep one foot in front of the other. Again, I was so glad of the company, as I was reduced to survival mode and could keep going only with the help of my ever-buoyant friends.

A little further down the path, Juan Pablo, the youngest, began complaining about the pain in his feet. He lay down on the road on his back while his cousin, Monica, massaged his feet. I wanted to lie down on the road too, but I knew I would never get up again. We were all vying to carry his pack to give him a chance to recover, but he doggedly refused. His aunt talked to him on her own, and after some food and a little TLC he made a rapid recovery. We were a fragile enough group of travelers between injuries and exhaustion. Even the weather was oppressive—we gave up putting on and taking off our rain gear and just walked in the rain, not really caring.

On this never-ending grey day we walked through more and more villages and developments for hikers: cafés, hostels, and boarding houses. The road became very busy as throngs of pilgrims overran us. There were also many "bicycle pilgrims," decked out with panniers, who flew past us. I was outraged to hear that a biker who was going too fast and couldn't stop had already hit Juan Pablo several days before. It all seemed too busy, fast, and frantic. Plus, the Camino was now all asphalt, with no respite for sore knees and tired tendons.

At this stage, Mariana, the inexhaustible aunt, had already fed us a number of times from her bottomless bag, but I was also raiding the automatic vending machines on the roadside for more energy. We were to meet Milli, the cousin who had been injured, at a place called Monte de Gozo (Hill of Joy), so called because it is the high point where medieval pilgrims would get their first view of Santiago. It was disappointing, however, as we couldn't see the city through the clouds and eucalyptus trees. I wasn't feeling much of that pilgrim joy. The tiny chapel of San Marcos was the only saving grace; we prayed here and got our pilgrim stamps.

We walked to the rusty monument of Pope John Paul II, where we met an exuberant Milli. She put us in good spirits, and we set out to walk the last four kilometers, an hour's walk into Santiago. I would love to say that they were joyous and pain free, but they were not (as befitting the Camino experience). Grueling, slow, and painful, it was an excruciating dragging of oneself into the city. It was now around one in the afternoon, and amazingly, we were in the suburbs of Santiago. I was also starving again. I told Mariana I had to eat, and again they were gracious enough to accompany me, right on the cusp of finishing. We had the special pilgrim's menu, not a spectacular meal but all the better for sharing it.

We set off again on the last two kilometers to the cathedral, the focal point. The streets wound uphill in a circular fashion to the old medieval center. We threaded our way through traffic lights and pedestrian crossings, now in silence, until we suddenly hit the old part of town. Then we walked downhill on the granite streets, through an archway, and out into the square in front of the impressive cathedral with its iconic facade. There was no great celebration or punching of the air. They were relieved, and I was battered and bewildered, like a sea survivor who is not used to being on dry land.

However, entering the cathedral was an awe-inspiring moment. The baroque facade and the Romanesque Pórtico da Gloria (Gate of Glory) are architectural wonders in themselves, but it was seeing the luminous baldachin ("cloth of gold") over the altar from the back of the nave that brought me to my knees. I felt like a medieval knight who had completed his quest and was now awed in the presence of his Lord. I was sure the former soldier St. Ignatius understood this image when he made his allegiance to Christ, his new Lord. Most of all, I could see the illuminated altar where I would place Donal's T-shirt, fulfilling the promise I had made to my siblings and finishing my monthlong quest. However, it was too much for me at this time. I got up off my knees to look for my companions.

Together, we made a beeline for the tomb of the apostle St. James (after whom the city is named, Sant Iago), underneath the main altar. We prayed a while there and then queued up to ascend the steps to embrace a statue of the apostle behind the altar. We also spent some time in the hushed reverence of the Blessed Sacrament chapel. I was impressed with the faith of my Latino friends, which was much stronger than mine. Having missed the pilgrim Mass for that day, we went to the pilgrim office to get our Compostelas, the official certificates for finishing the pilgrimage. I found the ritual moving, getting official recognition for being a pilgrim and for finishing, someone acknowledging the journey I had been on.

Afterward, the Alvarez family went off to their pensión, agreeing that we would meet the next day at the noon pilgrim Mass. I wanted to take some time to savor this moment, so I went back to the square, found a café that looked onto the cathedral, and had a cold beer. I appreciated everything—the day, the place, the people, my life, the gift of being here now. It felt great to sit there and just be, to watch all the comings and goings and marvel at it all. It was incredible that I had made it at all, and I was deeply grateful to God and all the myriad people who had helped me. I smiled to think of St. Ignatius looking down on me, and I thanked him for the gift of reflection that had seen me through some tough spots. However, I knew that I still had a lot of processing to do on this astoundingly complex and layered experience.

I eventually found the Jesuit community and was dismayed to find that because of an unfortunate mix-up in communications, they were not expecting me. The great welcome I was expecting for the conquering pilgrim-hero was cooler than I'd anticipated, and so I had a very low-key solitary evening unpacking. Everything was strewn around me, creased, filthy, and unwashed, pretty much the way I felt. I retired early for a much-needed sleep and collapsed unconscious into a dreamless world.

# 15
# Atonement

My eyes opened from way, way down in a pit. I had fallen into bed. A blanket of tiredness pressed down on me and kept me immobile. Something in the back of my head triggered a sort of psychic alarm that rung persistently—what was it about? Oh yes, it was about the pilgrim Mass at noon, which I really needed to be at. I struggled with the forces of gravity and sleep deprivation, pushing my legs and arms out from under the cover in what was a huge act of will. Eventually I sat there on the bed, unhappily bemoaning my fate of being so exhausted yet forced to get up on my first official day off in five weeks.

I remembered the days in the aftermath of Donal's death. I had prayed St. Patrick's Breastplate, a prayer of protection that I repeated now:

I arise today through the strength of heaven. . . . [137]

I thought about all the black mornings that those few words got me through, invoking the divine when I was incapable of action myself. I remembered Donal's depression and how he had not been able to "arise." However, I was now in Santiago de Compostela, named after the "field of stars"[138] and theater of divine promise. This was going to be a good day, a day of "rising." After showering, I put on Donal's old

T-shirt, which looked a sorry sight after all that time in the rucksack. I had been forced to wear it once when I ran out of clothes on the walk, but I felt Donal would understand. I took a moment on the steps of the Jesuit house, holding back tears. I already felt that this was going to be the moment I had been waiting for, the big release of the burden I had carried all the way from France. It was atonement, an offering of this symbol—the shirt—to erase all the shame and guilt. I knew I was offering myself to be transformed.[139]

Late, I raced down to the cathedral, which was only a few minutes away, hoping to be on the altar to concelebrate with all the other priests for the special noon pilgrim Mass. Even at twenty to the hour the cathedral was almost full with a variety of nationalities, voices, and costumes; a Latin American folk group sat in the front row with elaborate headdresses. I frantically searched for the sacristy, having to walk all the way around the high altar, which was thronged with tourists and camera lenses. I saw a medieval-dressed steward try to silence the boisterous crowd to no avail. Eventually I found the sacristy at the opposite end. Inside, sixteen priests from all over the world were already vesting to likewise concelebrate the Mass. My heart was beating fast as I slipped on my white alb, concealing Donal's T-shirt from everyone but me. The dean of the cathedral, Padre José Maria Diaz, was handing out assignments and coordinating the huge multicultural celebration. As the only native English speaker I was asked to do one of the Prayers of the Faithful and to read a small part of the Eucharistic Prayer.[140] In connection with the latter, he handed me a one-page leaflet that had the prayer printed out in English and my section highlighted in yellow:

> Lord, remember your Church throughout the world;
> Make us grow in love, together with Benedict our Pope,
> Julián our bishop, and all the clergy.

But as I looked below this prayer, my heart nearly stopped. I felt the words come up off the page toward me in a rush of emotion. What was written on this dog-eared sheet described exactly what I had come here for:

> Remember our brothers and sisters who have gone to their rest in the hope of rising again;
> Bring them and all the departed into the light of your presence.[141]

Specifically, it was the thought of Donal in the light of God's presence that brought a lump to my throat. As a family we had wrestled so long and hard with where our brother was—my sister had even asked at one point if he was in hell. It was shocking, but it named the horror our fear and anger had created—that there was no meaning, just pointless destruction. Now, however, I could scarcely believe my eyes. What my heart had told me for a long time, that Donal was with God in the "hope of the Resurrection," was now publicly proclaimed, here at the end of the road. I believed in God's mercy with all my broken heart.

However, I was mightily relieved that I had not been given those words to read. I would never have been able to say them in the state I was in: tired, emotional, and done-in, in all senses. The time came, and I processed out onto the altar with the other priests. Already the church was packed to the doors with pilgrims from over fifty countries, a sea of faces and colors.

The pilgrims who had received their Compostela (certificate) the day before had their countries of origin and their starting point announced at Mass. It was an awesome vista of diversity, so many dreams and personal struggles, and the key need to acknowledge the journey through ritual and rite. I heard my nationality read out and my starting point—Hendaye on the French border. What a journey!

I went through the Mass in a blur of emotion and memory; Donal's T-shirt seemed heavy and conspicuous even though no one else could see it. I thought about all the Masses that Donal had attended, all the football games where he would have worn this shirt, all the smiles and words that I had heard him exchange over his forty-one years. How much I had missed him, how much my life had fallen apart when he went, and how much I had struggled through these post-suicide years. I remembered one incident vividly that happened when we were young: he was hit by a stone on the head, and it opened a bloody wound. I had been so powerless and unable to protect him at the time—I wanted to be able to protect him now with this prayer. I hoped that this Santiago pilgrimage would finally lay all of this to rest, that this would be it. I was so tired of it all now.

> A widow who was distraught about her husband's suicide was afraid to approach St. John Vianney in Ars, France. Amazingly, he called out to her, "He is saved! Between the parapet of the bridge and the water he had time to make an act of contrition." The story speaks to the abundance of God's mercy for us all and the abiding hope in the Resurrection.

I pulled myself together to do the Prayer of the Faithful, going down to the lectern with six other priests who were talking in other tongues. I was conscious that all the English speakers would be listening in what was a sea of mainly Spanish. I began:

Through the intercession of St. James, the great protector of pilgrims;
     Make us strong in faith, and happy in hope, regardless of what comes.
     May our pilgrim journey continue in our normal lives back home.
     And sustain us so that we may finally reach the glory of God the Father.

Then there was a very erudite, long, and wordy homily by the Dean that I could just about follow in Spanish. I lamented what a lost opportunity it was to say something meaningful to this huge, largely secular gathering, who were then so receptive and open-hearted from the Road, many of whom would not darken the door of a church again. I wanted him to talk to

> In the Third Week of the *Spiritual Exercises,* St. Ignatius calls us to be with Jesus as we accompany him through the Passion. The challenge is to see how our own suffering and experiences of grief are present in Jesus, appreciating and feeling personally all he suffered for us.

people's experience of how they had been touched by Christ along the way. Then we were into the second part of the ceremony, the celebration of the Eucharist, where Jesus Christ offers his flesh and blood for the life of all. This spoke to me as never before: the very real suffering of Jesus in his humanity, the seeming triumph of evil on the cross, overcome by the self-giving love that expels all darkness.[142] The Camino was a small sharing in the suffering of Jesus, facing the darkness caused by suicide's reign, and rising through the light that is Christ. As the priest elevated the bread and the wine, I was conscious of the great sacrifices I and all pilgrims had made on the road to be here—hunger, pain, suffering—partaking in some small way in Christ's great self-giving in the Mass.

Now that the consecration was over, I knew that my prayer for the church and ministers was coming up fast. As I was seated at the back of the sanctuary in the old choir stalls, I started to make my way down to the altar early. Then, to my horror, a Polish priest stepped out from the right and got to the altar before me to read my bit. Reaching the altar, I paused behind him, unsure of what to do next. When the Polish priest finished, the Dean motioned to me to step in and read the next section—the very one I had not wanted to read. Through the element of surprise and not having time to prepare myself I was able to make it through those heartbreaking words, which were to be seared on my soul:

> Remember our brothers and sisters who have gone to their rest in
> the hope of rising again;
>   Bring them and all the departed into the light of your presence.

As I returned to my seat, I thought wryly that God has some sense of humor and that things do indeed happen for a reason, turning out much better than if we had planned them (the lesson of the Camino). I thought of the hope in those words, not just any hope, but the hope of the Resurrection, to be with Christ in the light of his presence. This is what I had longed for for so long for Donal.[143] I had known it on an intellectual level, but now I knew it within. As I made this powerful prayer, I felt like a prophet of old communicating God's message to an unbelieving world, a powerful witness for all who died through suicide: that God will redeem them by raising them up. Taking off my alb in the sacristy afterward, I felt relief and gratitude that the Camino was over wash through me. I could finally rest and recover.

Now that the Mass was over, I was really keen to see my Mexican friends who had carried me through the last days, and also others whom I had met on the way. The huge "Botafumeiro," the famous thurible used to bless pilgrims with incense (and disguise the bad odors emanating from many in the Middle Ages), did not make an appearance this time, disappointing many, and so the cathedral cleared out quickly. Outside in the always-busy Plaza del Obradoiro, I bumped into a number of familiar faces: the Belgian father of Mikael, the Dutch woman who had guided me to Güemes, and Anuk from the Netherlands. I felt the joy of meeting up again after absence and of having shared significant moments along the way. They asked me about Donal's T-shirt, and I proudly showed it off, bringing a tear to my eye. They had heard my voice over the sound system during the packed pilgrim Mass—some had not realized I was a priest until then. We arranged to go out for a meal that night. However, I still couldn't find the Alvarez family and was saddened by this.

Even though it had been a great day, with lots of precious moments, I couldn't help thinking, *Is that it?* I thought there would be something more dramatic; in many ways it was a bit of an anticlimax. As I prepared to go out for the evening, it felt strange not to be still earning my food on the road, wondering where I would sleep that night and always trying to "get there." Now that I had "got there," life was quite flat, humdrum, and ordinary—not at all what I thought it would be. That night the group of us who had walked together met for a celebration meal. Looking around, I knew it was unlikely that we would meet again. We had shared some important moments though, as well as a lot about our lives. Later we took to the quaint medieval streets of Santiago and gradually people drifted off to the rest of their lives.

# 16
# Journey to the End of the Earth

*Well, that's it*, I thought, closing the door of the Jesuit community in Santiago behind me. The high from the pilgrim Mass in the cathedral earlier that day was fading. I was looking forward to a quiet evening and a great sleep at last. This would be no ordinary sleep but the great healing-slumber marathon I craved. My head felt like the cockpit of a plane when all the warning lights were on: low fuel, equipment damaged, flying too low, wings fractured, immediate landing required.

In my mind I had already closed the door on the Camino experience and on the arduous, grueling trip it had been. I just wanted time off now, away from the intensity, from the sheer physicality, and especially from the unpredictable nature of what gets thrown at you. I felt like Ignatius returning home to Loyola to convalesce after being wounded at the Battle at Pamplona, craving a period of necessary recovery, restful healing, and protection from battles. I was in wind-down mode, already planning how I would quietly spend the final two days until my flight back to Ireland, and looking forward to normal life and what I had to do back home.

As I confidently breezed into the Jesuit dining room, I heard a familiar voice greet me in English. I was stunned. It took me a while to realize who it was—another Irish Jesuit friend of mine, Donal

Godfrey, who was based in the United States. It turned out that he had been doing the Camino Francés from Sarria to Santiago (115 kilometers) over a week, finishing in Santiago the day before. Neither of us had realized we were on the same path, just one day apart, until our paths intersected at the Jesuit community.

After the meal, we walked and talked, intuitively engaged in "faith sharing" or spiritual conversation,[144] familiar to us both from Jesuit community life. I relished the chance to do this with a friend; it seemed the perfect ending to the Camino odyssey. I was horrified to hear of his encounter with bedbugs (common enough in the hostels) and the visible weal-like marks they had left. I told him about my assorted medical problems and how I had just scraped through.

Then Donal floated the idea of going to Finisterre, which literally means "the end of the world," the next day. Finisterre, on the western-most point of the coast, is the unofficial end of the Camino. I found myself torn, conscious of my much-desired sleep. Though I could feel the old pilgrim call stirring in the pit of my stomach, I pushed it down. After all, I had promised myself that I wouldn't do any more walking, would not endure any more painful challenges, that it was just all rest and relaxation from here on. The idea of going to the place where the Camino met the ocean did not really appeal to me. *I have done my Camino process and more than enough*, I thought. *The last thing I need is another trek.* I had finished what I had come to do, to deliver the T-shirt to Santiago, and I had gotten everything I was going to get from the experience. However, my Jesuit training had taught me to avoid making quick decisions. Looking at the other side, there were some good things about going to Finisterre: the chance to spend more time with Donal, to do some more debriefing on the Camino, and to be in travel mode again, even if it was on the bus. It was to be Donal's last day before returning to the United States too, so that was another factor in favor of going.

I knew what my body wanted (R&R), but I knew that I needed to go through the Ignatian decision-making process of discernment. Meaning to sift or to sort, discernment[145] is akin to gold panning, where the gravel has to be shaken through a sieve to reveal the nuggets of precious metal. Essentially, it's separating the gold from the dross, the light from the dark, the good from the bad in human experience. So, I put myself to discerning what the best thing to do was—asking what was God really wanting of me here and praying for freedom. On one level I knew I wanted to rest and stay put, but this didn't feel quite right. Part of the problem, I realized, was that I found it difficult to be free and detached as Ignatius would have wanted. As I had promised myself this hard-earned rest and had looked forward to it so much during the last four weeks, I had become attached to it, and a little inflexible about it. I wasn't free anymore; I was chained to staying put.

> Spiritual conversation is a form of prayer in which our communication with God is made real through other people. It is a style of talking and dialogue that prioritizes respect, listening, and collective discernment. Spiritual conversation can bring us closer to God as we share our insights and experiences with one another.

These were some of the "unfreedoms" and resistances that Ignatius mentions in his Rules for Discernment.[146] On one level it was understandable to crave rest after five weeks of tough exertion, but on another it was a lack of inner freedom—I would have plenty of time to rest when I got home, and it really wasn't going to make much difference whether I went on the trip or not. However, I had a strange feeling that God wanted me to go on this trip for reasons that were not clear to me. Still, I grumbled and moaned internally like a load-bearing Sherpa asked to make a push for a higher summit.[147] Finally, I said yes to Donal and to the trip to the "end of the world" and felt lighter and more positive, confirmation of what I hoped would be a good decision.

So it was that we were on the early bus out of Santiago, heading due west for the Atlantic coast and the Cape of Finisterre. Steeped in legend and myth, this place was believed to have been the westernmost point of the Iberian Peninsula (in fact, Cabo da Roca in Portugal is the most westerly). Made of hard crystalline rock, Finisterre plunges into the *Mare Tenebrosum* (or the "dark sea," as the Atlantic was known). It sent a shiver down my back to know that the locals call it the "Death Coast" (Costa da Morte) because of all the shipwrecks and fatalities that occurred there over the years. The place sounded dramatic and almost dangerous.

I closed my eyes briefly on the two-hour coach journey and, not for the first time, thanked God for a safe arrival and for the end of an epic trip. The clouds rolled in as I looked out the window, and it began to rain. My first thought went to my fellow pilgrims who were out in this weather on their last three days' walk to the sea. As we careered along by coastal towns, beaches, and rocky outcrops, I saw how very different this land was to the inland Asturian Camino and the bucolic meadows I had walked.

Then I saw them: little isolated groups of hikers struggling against the wind in flapping capes, walking on rough broken trails that had the tell-tale yellow-arrow Camino markers. I felt a great love for these unknown people on their coastal pilgrim way and a pang of regret not to be walking, but mostly a sense of relief at being swept along at speed. I never realized how little I appreciated transport and technology. Now that I had walked so much, I knew what it meant.

We arrived into a wet and drizzly Finisterre, and all romantic notions were dispelled. The city looked more like Limerick on a wet day. We sat in a fast-food café, surrounded by other dripping tourists, sipping hot chocolate and eating local sandwiches. We looked out on the persistent rain and low clouds over the harbor, which stripped it of any charm or beauty. I wondered whether I should have come. We were in danger of falling into a low mood and dull conversation, so we hurried out of the café and hit on the idea of walking the four kilometers out to the lighthouse on the cape. At least we would get to walk the last, ultimate section of the Camino where it met the wild Atlantic. So off we set, in a low, grey drizzle, for the cape at the end of the world.

This was a very short walk in comparison to what we had done to date, but it felt interminable. The road continued to rise up into pine forests that seemed to draw down the clouds. To our left we could hear and smell the sea but, frustratingly, couldn't see it. It was a real walk into the unknown, into a darkness of sorts, and a test of faith. I felt distinctly uneasy and troubled. One of the books I had found on my brother Donal's bedside table after his death was *The Cloud of Unknowing*.[148] The key insight of the book was that God could not be known by knowledge or intellect but rather through a "dart of longing love" from the heart. In many ways my post-suicide life had taken on this aspect of not knowing what lay ahead, not being able to see clearly and having to blindly trust. *Here I am again*, I thought, grimly trudging up an endless hill into the mist, not feeling much love in my heart and having misgivings as to whether it was worth it. Again, the dogged determination of my fellow Jesuit Donal kept me going.

Things started to appear out of the mist: first several hikers, then a statue of a female pilgrim clutching a bunch of flowers beside the road. It seemed unbearably sad in the swirling mist, somewhat funereal. I shuddered at the thought. Then we came across a huge stone cross, embedded in a platform of rock. With the billowing mist and in the half-light this looked decidedly macabre, and we took some dramatic photos. Suddenly we came upon some small shops and then a small café with people huddled inside, and finally a huge, grim white-and-brown building emerged from the mist. This low, squat building operated as a hotel, with an octagonal granite lighthouse located behind it. As we moved on to the rocky point behind the lighthouse, many meters above the Atlantic, we saw figures moving about on the headland in the mist, with small fires billowing smoke at their feet. This seemed to be the height of bizarreness in what had been a strange day. They were pilgrims engaged in a peculiar ritual of burning their clothes at the end of the Camino. Enwrapped in a certain cathartic intensity, this scene made riveting watching, despite the acrid smoke. Nonetheless, it felt like we were intruding on their privacy, and we retreated, having no business there.

As we turned around to go home in the rain, a certain idea slowly but insistently imposed itself: *There is an item of clothing I have to burn, and now I understand why I am here and the significance of this seemingly wasted day.* It was a terrifying idea in some ways as I grasped the import of it and what it would cost me. To burn Donal's T-shirt, the last connection I had to him in this world, was to totally let go of my grasp on him. But I could not deny this little moment of revelation and the clarity with which it appeared to me as being a sound idea, an idea from God. Ignatius defined consolation, the movement toward the light, as "any increase of our faith, our hope, and our love. A deep-down peace comes from our living life as 'being in our Father's house.'"[149] It seemed to me that this was what I was experiencing now, this sense of great peace, even amid feelings of fear and loss.

This deeper sense of calm, of quiet self-possession and interior joy, was to last all day. When I explained my idea to my friend Donal, he was very supportive of it, though he had to go back that evening. Saying good-bye to him was not easy—now I was alone with my conflicting emotions. I booked a cheap room in Finisterre, precariously located on the top floor of an impossibly narrow house with steep steps but which had a panoramic view of the harbor. I could see many fishing boats tied up below, though Monte Pindo across the bay was obscured by clouds. That evening I visited the castle of San

Carlos, perched on a rocky promontory, and, though we had a great tour guide, I couldn't concentrate on anything. Even though there were other pilgrims I knew in town, I decided to eat alone in the guest house and gather my courage for what I knew would be a difficult day.

I awoke at 6:30 a.m. with the light penetrating the flimsy curtains. It was a bright, clear morning in Finisterre on the Atlantic coast. The turquoise dawn that greeted my tired eyes was in such contrast to the drizzle and mist of the previous day. I missed my friend Donal, who had gone back to Santiago to catch his flight, and I felt very much alone in this unknown territory, the Camino beyond the Camino. Fixed in my head was what I knew I had to do from having observed other pilgrims engage in their bizarre clothes-burning ritual the day before. The finality of it was terrifying.

I lifted my rucksack as I had done countless times in the last forty days, except this time it was strangely light; there was only one item of clothing in it, a Barcelona FC T-shirt. Placing it inside, I had an image of my brother Donal playing football, happy and well. It hurt to remember.

> Ignatius wrote that in doing penance, our external act should mirror our internal desire to ask God for some special favor or grace. A pilgrimage embodies an explicit prayer.

My rucksack seemed a fitting way to transport this precious garment to its final resting place. I left at 7:30 a.m. on a fasting stomach, nothing new for me, but somehow it felt more important here.[150] There was so much I desired: forgiveness, a release from guilt and grief, and, for my brother, Donal, especially, peace of body and soul. No other pilgrims were on the road, unlike the previous day when there had been many. I marveled at the continually evolving sunrise in its interplay with the clouds. I dreaded what lay ahead yet felt called to carry it out. I prayed for strength.

On the way up the hill I passed the church of Santa María das Areas, a twelfth-century Romanesque church that we had visited the previous day. I had their prayer card in my hand with a graphic image of the suffering Christ figure by an unknown fourteenth-century sculptor. It vividly portrays his last moments before death. A super realistic portrayal of pain and agony, the image could have been gruesome and macabre—if it were the end—and yet it was a symbol of hope and strength for me now.

Strengthened by this, I pressed on toward the lighthouse on the cape, this far-flung finger of land thrust into the Atlantic. It was as dramatic a place as I have ever seen, all the more poignant for the ritual I was about to perform. I got to the end of the path behind the lighthouse and started off down the rough path among the scorched rocks, marked by other pilgrim offerings. I suddenly realized that I didn't have any matches or a lighter. I had presumed that the little shop back up the road would be open, but, of course, it wasn't at this hour. I was shocked. I stared out to the sea, disconsolate, making out distant whitecaps. *What a stupid mistake*, I thought, *that such a simple thing would sink my whole plan.*

After a few moments I heard a noise behind me and saw another hiker making his way through the rocks. He was French, but we communicated easily, a nonverbal intuition that understood the important nature of what has to be done. He lent me his lighter and then discreetly moved away to give me space.

I held the T-shirt for a moment, torn within, as this was the last fragment of Donal that I possessed. This would be it, no more. I knew well what this sacred rite was: a letting go of my brother, of my grief, and of the traumatic last few years that had been so awful. There was something comforting about my grief, my pain, and my hold on Donal, which I was putting in jeopardy here. It was easier to live in the dusty, memory-filled rooms of the past than to open up to new air and new life. I had identified with my mourning for so long, it had become part of who I was. The idea of losing this security and comfort blanket was terrifying.

I wanted to stop, to go home, to flee, but at a deeper level I knew I was bound to carry out this ritual of fire. I was trusting in a future of hope and, critically, in my belief that I would see my dear Donal again. I wouldn't need any earthly reminders of him, as we would be having a face-to-face encounter in heaven. Committing myself, I knew I couldn't undo the decision I had made initially to come.[151] It was an enormous act of will to put the flame to the Barcelona FC T-shirt that I had carried all the way from the French border, some eight hundred kilometers away.

And then—the anticlimax—it wouldn't light! The material was too heavy, and the wind was too strong. I tried a more sheltered spot between two rocks but to no avail. I looked up to see where my French Good Samaritan was, but he was nowhere to be seen; I was worried about using up all his lighter fluid.

Eventually I hit on the idea of using a tissue as a crude tinder to get the T-shirt burning. Fortunately it worked, and within seconds I had a steady flame from the tissue that created enough heat to melt the heavy fabric. Melt is what it did, turning into globules of molten fabric, spilling onto the ground. It happened so rapidly, disappearing before my eyes. I wanted to hold onto the last familiar remnants. I was alarmed at how quickly it all broke down and dissolved.

Suddenly, unable to hold the shirt any longer, I let it fall into a fiery heap. I felt myself disintegrating. I fell into sobs beside a nearby rock, in a fetal position from the emotional meltdown. It hurt intensely; these were racking sobs that came from the bottom of my soul—all that grief, all that anger, all that loss, all that pain, everything that had nowhere to go. Now it all came out into the Iberian light. This really was the end of the road, the desperate plea of an exhausted pilgrim unable to bear the load. The black scorched rocks and remnants of burnt clothing seemed a fitting environment for this purging of the past, a veritable wasteland of memory and bitter regrets. I had been drinking from a terribly bitter cup, brought to my knees with suffering. Once the spasms came to a natural end, I dusted myself off, feeling empty and spent. I was barely able to stand, and struggled to believe that some of the darkness had passed and that some new hope had been born.

Afterward I went and sat in the sun with my empty rucksack. Gradually, I began to feel well despite the ordeal I had been through. A fellow pilgrim kindly agreed to take my photo, and it reveals a face aglow, at peace and transformed. I sat there for a long time, just being. It was God's time now, kairos time, outside of chronological time, when extraordinary things happen. This experience of living in God's love freely given was deeply consoling and satisfying.[152] I had a strong sense of that "giftedness," grace, or blessing as I had not earned or deserved this in any way. I felt the whole journey on the Camino had been a preparation for this moment, a stripping down of the ego and self-centeredness, and an openness to providence and what the moment brought. This was the greatest gift I could have hoped for, totally unexpected, literally at the last moment, and all the more welcome.

On the way back to Finisterre I spied a rare sandy beach down at the bottom of the endless cliffs. I made my way down some steps and changed. The plunge into the green surf of the Atlantic took my breath away. The cold sent a tingle through my synapses, and I felt new life surge within me. A few strokes out into the Bay of Biscay, and the years and the tears fell away—it felt like I was born again. I thrashed the salty brine with my fists in pure joy. Back on the beach I found a standpipe where I could wash off the salt. Ignatius once said that God showers down gifts and blessings on us like a waterfall. As I washed, it struck me that all I have and all that I am has been given to me, and the Camino has been God's gift, custom-designed for me.

Undeniably the Spirit was speaking to me directly. The message was stop trying to go it alone with your own striving and solo efforts; lay back and trust God, trust the universe and the road to deliver you what you need.

I could now see the invitation to get off the mad wheel of competitiveness and busyness that the world promotes. I knew the importance of walking my own Camino at my own pace. This meant not being distracted by others, keeping my own quiet and humble goals. I understood I would get there in God's time and through God's love, by trusting and following the urgings within. I knew in my bones that God works through all things, people, circumstances, and events, to indicate his love for me. It is only through my response of gratitude, humility, and love that life can be lived authentically.

On the bus back to Santiago, my heart fairly sang. The Galician countryside was dazzling in the afternoon sun, such a contrast to the bleak drizzle of the day before. I marveled at how a life can change in one itinerant month or even in one dramatic day on the coast. I could feel God's love for me made tangible in these last hours, but also on the enlightening Camino and

> The Fourth Week of the *Spiritual Exercises* is an experience of resurrection, a sudden heartfelt realization of God's transforming love. Ignatius would have called this experience deep consolation, being on fire with God's love and realizing that everything is a freely given gift.

in my whole life. In the light of this radiance, I prayed for forgiveness for all my mistakes and for the courage to press on into whatever new life God had in store for me. Like Ignatius did at one key moment, I asked, *What kind of a new life is this that we are now beginning?* [153] For the first time in a long time, I had real hope.

On arriving in Santiago again, I was content to amble around the old town, to be in the cathedral and to catch up with some friends. Just before I left for home, the Jesuit superior, Father Amor, told me, "I think you really got the Camino thing." I had to agree with him, although I rather think it got me. Walking the road to Santiago had stripped me of my illusions and prepared me for a new awakening.

It was a considerably leaner, lighter, and transformed person who finally arrived in Galway on a lovely July evening. I walked with my friends through the Spanish Arch, appropriately enough, and they accompanied me the last few hundred yards to my home. After some customary tea and scones and a lot of talk, I made it to my own room. Collapsing into bed, I was in heaven.

# Epilogue

There is a saying in Santiago that if you walk five times around the cathedral you will meet all your friends from the Camino. I was particularly keen to meet the Alvarez family, whom I feared might have left Spain at this point, but also all the many others I had met along the way. The day after I arrived back from Finisterre, I made my last visit to the cathedral. I didn't even have to walk once around it. No sooner had I left the Jesuit residence in Santiago than I ran into a couple of my former students from the school where I was chaplain. They had just finished the Camino too, a few days behind me, and there was lots of catching up to be done.

Later that day, I popped into the busy cathedral for a quick good-bye prayer and was delighted to meet my friends from Tineo, the eighty-year-old Frenchman Anton, and his Belgian helper, Frederick. I talked animatedly with Frederick for a few moments in the aisle, but Anton, whom I joined in the pews, said nothing—he just embraced me and held my gaze for what seemed an eternity. Even without a common language, this was a beautiful moment of communion that only shared experience on the Road can give.

Outside the cathedral on a side street I ran into a jubilant Sarah, who had just finished the Camino. She proudly showed me the new boots she had gotten the day after I left her in Lugo. She hugged me and introduced me to a Dutch friend as "the guy who saved me." It did me much good to see her so well and on the other side of so many difficulties.

Just when I thought I couldn't bear any more of this emotional intensity, and time was pressing, I ran into a familiar group of Latino faces at the north gate. I was thrilled to meet the Alvarez family on their way to the airport. They greeted me so warmly, and I felt so strongly like they were family that I was in tears. I was trying to find the words to thank them in Spanish, but they shortcut this attempt by presenting me with a very Mexican gift, a card called a *ramillete espiritual* (spiritual bouquet), which outlined all the prayers, penances, and Masses they would offer for me. Once again, their generosity overtook my attempts to thank them. I was reduced to an incoherent, blubbering wreck. I do believe it was one of the best presents I ever received.

Back at the Jesuit residence, I packed my tired-looking hiking gear. Unfortunately I wasn't able to take my faithful yellow backpack as cabin baggage, so I tenderly placed it in the storeroom for recycling. It had served me well, and I hoped it would serve someone else well too—another lesson in detachment. As the plane took off from Santiago, the Camino was laid out below, and I felt that I had left a huge weight there too. I prayed that this new life before me, whatever it was, would be lived like a pilgrim, reflective and filled with gratitude.

On the final bus journey back home to Galway, I savored the lush Irish landscape as if arriving for the first time—I was tingling with the delicious anticipation of homecoming. Walking from the bus station, I felt like I was on another leg of the Camino, focused on passing through the city, as people brushed past with their cares and concerns. However, I felt an enormous sense of joy and contentment in simply being alive. A small number of Jesuits, friends, and family gathered to meet me at the Spanish Arch on the banks of the river Corrib in Galway. I fell into their embraces and affection, the returning pilgrim but hardly a hero. I solemnly placed a scallop shell around their necks, a small ritual of inclusion in the Camino journey that would be theirs to walk one day. We walked the last few hundred meters together to the Jesuit house. I was home at last. Getting into my own bed had never felt so delicious and luxurious as it did for that magnificent and much-anticipated sleep.

The next morning, I went for a walk on the Salthill promenade and met an old friend of mine. I was still full of enthusiasm and bonhomie on the homecoming high. "I did the Camino!" I proudly proclaimed.

"Did you walk all of it?"

"Well, I had to take the bus a few times, but that wasn't actually the important thing. . . ." I answered, gearing up to share my many and varied insights.

To my dismay, he cut me off: "Oh now," he said, "you know Michael from Spiddal, he is over sixty, and he walked the whole thing last year." It was a none-too-subtle putdown. I was shocked that this was the end of the conversation. The competition ethos runs deep and wide, I realized, not only on the trail but in the heart of ordinary life. I felt like I had been judged and had come up wanting and was left frustrated and disappointed.

As I sat on my own later, overlooking the bay, I ruefully remembered that I had had a lot of preparation for this. I could see both Ignatius and Donal laughing at the irony of the situation. The whole point of the exercise was to become free of people's expectations or approval, and here I was, caught again. Very soon I felt my resistance thaw out, and I began to laugh with them. *The learning never stops,* I thought. At that the sun came out from behind a cloud, and the waters of Galway Bay glistened in response.

I reflected that the core message for me was to be grateful for all I had received and not to compare myself to anyone else. A Jesuit friend of mine used to say, "Compare and despair." It looked like I was going to need some more time on the road with this one. With that I took up my bag and faced into the westerly breeze, seeing the flinty shine of the Burren across from me. I knew then that few would understand what had happened on that long month in Spain—I didn't even know how I would begin to communicate it. I resolved to let it mature within me until the time was right. This book is the fruit of that process.

# Acknowledgments

I would like to thank my family, including my network of cousins and all those who helped us grieve the loss of Donal. Special thanks to the Killen family. I'm grateful to the many friends and colleagues who encouraged me on the Camino, those who posted messages on my blog, and especially those who sponsored me to walk for Console, the suicide-bereavement charity. I would like to thank in a special way my Jesuit family who supported me all the way; this took the form of much-needed accommodation on the Camino in Burgos, Oviedo, and Santiago. Particular thanks must go to José de Pablo, SJ, who was my trip planner and tour guide. Donal Godfrey, SJ, played a very providential role in Santiago, for which I shall be forever grateful.

There were many other nameless people on the Camino who selflessly gave of their time and generosity to help me through. I will never forget the solidarity of the pilgrims I met on the road. Also the volunteers, hospitaleros, shopkeepers, bartenders, chemists, and many doctors who helped on the Way, and those who just pointed the direction with a smile, not even saying a word.

I am indebted to Pat Coyle, director of Jesuit Communications, who encouraged and helped me with the initial proposal and early stages of writing. Special thanks to Karen Rossignol and Conall O'Cuinn, SJ, who reviewed early drafts of the chapters and gave me invaluable feedback and suggestions. My gratitude also goes to Henry Grant, SJ, who gave me valuable editorial advice, to Nicole Stapff for her help on translations, and to Peter Wedderburn for his proofreading. Thanks to Paul Kelly and Console, who have been there for me and many others at tough moments.

This book was written "on the move," in a pilgrim fashion, so thanks to the generosity of various Jesuit communities in Ireland (St. Ignatius, Galway; and Peter Faber, Belfast) and Canada (Regis Formation Community, the Jesuit Curia, Toronto; St. John's, Newfoundland; and St. Ignatius, Guelph [the hermitage]). Thanks to Tony O'Riordan, SJ, my constant companion for the original pilgrim insights on 1994's walk. Finally, thanks to Orpen Press and Loyola Press, who have been supportive and skilled and always encouraged the best writing and production values.

# Notes

1. *Donal*, from the Irish word *Domhnall*, means "world mighty." *Donal* is its anglicized form. It was the ninth most popular name in early Ireland (Donnchadh O'Corrain and Fidelma Maguire, *Gaelic Personal Names* [Dublin: Academic Press, 1981]).

2. Joseph N. Tylenda, SJ, *A Pilgrim's Journey: The Autobiography of Ignatius of Loyola* (Collegeville, MN: Liturgical Press, 1991), No. 8, 14–15.

3. Michael Ivens, SJ, *An Approach to Saint Ignatius of Loyola*, ed. Joseph Munitiz, SJ (Oxford: Way Books, 2008), 8–9.

4. It was intriguing the way Ignatius found the spirit in his affectivity, or feelings. He had to have time out, recuperation, and solitude in order for these to surface. See Michael O'Sullivan, SJ, "Trust Your Feelings, but Use Your Head: Discernment and the Psychology of Decision Making," *Studies in the Spirituality of Jesuits* 22, no. 4, 1990.

5. References to the Spiritual Exercises are based on David L. Fleming, SJ, *Draw Me into Your Friendship—The Spiritual Exercises: A Literal Translation and a Contemporary Reading* (St. Louis: Institute of Jesuit Sources, 1996). The abbreviation *SE* is used throughout this book as an abbreviation for the *Spiritual Exercises*.

6. Described in Brendan McManus, SJ, "Ignatian Pilgrimage: The Inner Journey—Loyola to Manresa on Foot," *The Way* 49, no. 3 (July 2010).

7. A bereaved father (played by Martin Sheen) decides to walk the Way of St. James in honor of his son (www.theway-themovie.com).

8. Margaret Silf, *Inner Compass: An Invitation to Ignatian Spirituality* (Chicago: Loyola Press, 1998), 51–52.

9. Surprisingly, Ignatius encouraged great desires. He believed God is in our deepest desires, not our superficial ones. Pilgrimage and journeying allow us to go deeper so that we distinguish what is valuable for us and what is dross (see Silf, *Inner Compass*, chapter 8).

10. That is, as a seeker or wanderer. It means cutting ties and leaving home, leaving the past behind, to be open to something new and hopefully enlightening. "Outwardly becoming a wandering and unknown stranger and inwardly, on the unknown road towards one's true self, towards God," wrote Peter Muller and Angel Fernandez de Aranguiz in *Every Pilgrim's Guide to Walking to Santiago de Compostela*, trans. Laurie Dennett (Norwich: Canterbury Press, 2010), xxv.

11. Ignatius reflected his self-understanding when he referred to himself as "the pilgrim" in relating his life story. See Tylenda, *A Pilgrim's Journey*, xiv.

12. It is very sobering to realize that backpack weight is the key criteria for injury-free walking, and that 10 percent of your body weight is the ideal. Inevitably, compromises have to be made. This radical one cost a few nights' sleep but was probably worth it overall (see www.urcamino.com/camino-frances/what-to-carry).

13. Dockside poem in Hondarribia, Gipuzkoa, Basque Country; my translation.

14. *Camino* translates as "way" in English, which seems to capture my search for closure and a reconfiguration of faith. Early Christians also described themselves as following "the Way" in the Acts of the Apostles.

15. Also known as the Examen of Consciousness, this prayer is a key one in Ignatius's *Spiritual Exercises* (*SE* 43), because it helps you process the day and reflect on where the Spirit has been in your daily life (see www.loyolapress.com/how-can-i-pray-try-the-daily-examen.htm).

16. I couldn't help but think of the Gospel of John, 15:1–17, where Jesus is the true vine and God is the gardener who prunes the branches for greater fruitfulness.

17. One of the Spiritual Exercises has you imagine that you are selected by a great king or leader to be part of his or her team, which means giving up all luxuries and selfishness in order to be part of the world-changing divine vision (*SE* 91–100).

18. This is simply a state of mindfulness, being present to your body and the moment (see http://goodlifezen.com/zen-and-the-art-of-walking).

19. Loyola is also the starting point for the Ignatian walking pilgrimage, the Camino Ignaciano, which I had done twenty years previously (see http://caminoignaciano.org/en).

20. Discernment is "an inner compass that shows each of us the path of intimacy with God," Monty Williams, SJ, *The Gift of Spiritual Intimacy: Following the Spiritual Exercises of Saint Ignatius* (Toronto, ON: Novalis, 2009), 28.

21. A "spiritual exercise" is awareness, meditation, or reflection, any practice that helps increase openness to the Spirit (*SE* 1).

22. David L. Fleming, SJ, *Draw Me into Your Friendship—The Spiritual Exercises: A Literal Translation and a Contemporary Reading* (St. Louis: Institute of Jesuit Sources, 1996), 5.

23. This is the theological belief that nothing is beyond the healing love of Christ.

24. Detachment is freedom from addictive or damaging dependencies (Margaret Silf, *Inner Compass: An Invitation to Ignatian Spirituality* [Chicago: Loyola Press, 1998], 141–169).

25. I wanted to live the Ignatian ideal of leadership through self-awareness and self-reflection, staying true to one's own values and principles through being "detached," or "indifferent," despite what others are doing. See Chris Lowney, *Heroic Leadership* (Chicago: Loyola Press, 2003), 27–31.

26. The name comes from the Sanskrit word for "god" or "deity."

27. Originally, I thought I would be swimming every day on this coastal route, but this would be the only time.

28. We belong to God and other things come second; otherwise, they can get in the way, disturb our "balance," and make us slaves to them, e.g., addictions (*SE* 23).

29. Matthew 5:14: the light has to shine unobstructed in order for us to see the way.

30. Ignatius invites us to face our fears, make discerned decisions, and act against unhealthy attachments to achieve genuine freedom (*SE* 149–155).

31. Eric Walker and Chris Lennie, *Los Caminos del Norte, A: Ruta de la Costa: Irún-Villaviciosa No. 1 (Pilgrim Guides to Spain)* (London: The Confraternity of Saint James, 2010).

32. NLP is an alternative therapy for the treatment of all sorts of psychological and physical problems.

33. Ignatius was intent on killing a "Moor" who he thought had insulted Our Lady. The saint could not decide what to do, so he dropped the reins and let the mule he was riding decide. Fortunately, his mule took another path than that of the Moor. This divesting of responsibility was clearly not discernment, but it probably drove Ignatius to find a better way to make decisions subsequently.

34. It is crucial to identify those compulsions or negative attachments that stop us from being free (*SE* 15 and 179).

35. The insight is "give up control, let go." See http://ignatianeducator.com/tag/xavier/.

36. In the *Spiritual Exercises,* Ignatius suggests that you ask directly for the "grace" or desire that you seek (*SE* 48).

37. This is the quintessential Camino greeting, meaning "Have a great walk."

38. The irony was that Ignatius's devastating injury was also to his leg, and he always walked with a limp after that. This physical injury that forced him to recuperate facilitated his conversion.

39. Reflectively reviewing the events of the day reveals another layer of meaning (*SE* 43).

40. In the fundamental Exercise, the Principle and Foundation (*SE* 23), Ignatius has a curious phrase that we should not "prefer health to sickness." He lists it under things relating to indifference or detachment (being free of), but it is challenging to be able to accept illness freely or to accept that it could be part of a divine plan.

41. One of Ignatius's particularly useful guidelines for decisions is never to go back on a decision that was made when you were in consolation (i.e., when in good shape, balanced, and free of influences) (*SE* 318).

42. Flowing from the Exercises is the technique of spiritual direction, actively listening to help the other find freedom to choose well. See William A. Barry, SJ, and William J. Connolly, SJ, *The Practice of Spiritual Direction* (New York: Seabury Press, 1982), 3–12.

43. He was the illustrator for a Spanish book about the Jesuits: www.salterrae.es/catalogo/pdf/En_compania_de_Jesus.pdf.

44. The Spiritual Exercises are normally done in a retreat house, a secluded setting, but Ignatius does make provision for adapting them to different situations. The Camino would be an obvious one (*SE* Annotations 18 and 20).

45. Intriguingly, we are told, "The greatest consolation he received at this time was from gazing at the sky and the stars . . ." (Joseph N. Tylenda, SJ, *A Pilgrim's Journey: The Autobiography of Ignatius of Loyola* [Collegeville, MN: Liturgical Press, 1991], 17).

46. Ever the pragmatist, Ignatius has us consider the pros and cons of a decision, especially seeing it from the opposite point of view to our own (*SE* 181).

47. *Adios* literally means "to God." It is an abbreviation of *A Dios vais* ("You're going to God," meaning to the kingdom of Heaven).

48. Ignatius would have understood freedom as "freedom for" living life fully and "freedom from" unhealthy attachments, such as compulsions or addictions.

49. "Heart burning within me" is a reference to the disciples listening to Jesus on the road to Emmaus, but it also captures a particularly Jesuit way of praying. See Michael Harter, SJ, ed., *Hearts on Fire: Praying with Jesuits* (Chicago: Loyola Press, 2004).

50. Echoing the Suscipe, a prayer of great affection and gratitude at the end of the *Exercises* (*SE* 234).

51. Ignatian freedom is about freely accepting any conditions or circumstances as gifts without being limited by preconceptions (*SE* 21).

52. Ignatius advocated giving people the benefit of the doubt and assuming they have positive intentions (*SE* Annotation 22).

53. The voluntary body Asociaciones de Amigos del Camino de Santiago provides hospitality in many hostels (www.caminosantiago.org/cpperegrino/comun/inicio.asp).

54. This is classic desolation—dissonant feelings that lead one away from God (*SE* 317).

55. "Try to be like a balance at equilibrium, without leaning to either side" (*SE* 179).

56. Joseph A. Munitiz, SJ, "St. Ignatius of Loyola and Severe Depression," *The Way* 44, no. 3 (July 2005): 58–59.

57. A good idea taken to excess distorts and becomes unhelpful. We can be misled by great intentions and holy thoughts that are not really genuine (*SE* 332).

58. Ignatius had a section of the *Spiritual Exercises* called "Rules for Discernment," which were practical, distilled guidelines on decision making derived from his own experiences (*SE* 313–336).

59. The bad spirit is disguised as an angel of light to deceive the good person (*SE* 332).

60. We need to examine the whole sequence of thoughts to see where they soured (*SE* 333 and 334).

61. Gerald O'Mahony, SJ, illustrates balancing moods by using the image of a boat having to continually adjust while crossing a tidal estuary. The tide could be incoming or outgoing, so to compensate correctly, one must be aware of the tidal flow, i.e., how the person is being pulled (*Finding the Still Point* [Guildford, England: Eagle Publishing, 1992], 25–28).

62. Seeing everything as a gift comes from realizing how much I have received, and it opens my heart (*SE* 233).

63. Camino hostels are also known as *refugios*, from the Latin *refugium*, meaning "refuge" or "shelter." The name is seen as an allusion to Nuestra Señora del Refugio, or Our Lady of Refuge, one of the names for the Virgin Mary in the Christian tradition.

64. Seeking to cultivate an "attitude of gratitude" (Brian J. Lehane, SJ, "Attitude of Gratitude: The Examen Prayer of St. Ignatius," *Partners*, www.jesuits-chgdet.org/wp-content/uploads/2011/03/Partners_FA09.Spirituality.pdf) (*SE* 32–43).

65. From an Ignatian point of view, caught at an existential low point, I was being pulled by different "spirits" and struggling to stay faithful to the rules of discernment (*SE* 316–336).

66. From an Ignatian point of view, this was an experience of consolation, a "deep-down peace" and a trusting attitude (*SE* 316).

67. This is the key Ignatian question of meaning, but it probably betrays some frustration and desolation here, i.e., temptations to despair, undermining the decision made, and giving up (*SE* 317).

68. Knowing I was in need, I asked for the strength and patience to get me through (*SE* 48).

69. Brendan McManus, SJ, "Surviving Suicide," *The Furrow* 61, no. 2 (February 2010): 98–108.

70. This is better known by its Latin title, *agere contra*, a form of Ignatian asceticism necessary for spiritual progress. Ivens outlines well the priority of finding a mean, or balance. See Michael Ivens, SJ, *Understanding the Spiritual Exercises* (Leominster, England: Gracewing, 1998) (*SE* 13, 317, 322).

71. The enforced time-out allowed many issues and stumbling blocks to arise and be addressed in prayer, freeing me to move onward in my journey. See Carol A. Smith and Eugene F. Merz, *Moment by Moment: A Retreat in Everyday Life* (Notre Dame, IN: Ave Maria Press, 2005).

72. The ideal of walking the perfect Camino with no deviations, doctors, or assistance.

73. I realized I was being unfairly attacked and responding unreflectively in kind. I knew I had to act against this (*SE* 13) to restore my peace, balance, and goodwill toward her.

74. Ignatius has this image about ourselves as a military fortress, and that we are attacked by the enemy at our weakest point, where our defenses are low. For me it was the guilt trip about my injuries and difficulties. An impenetrable fortress seemed to be the best defense against this aggressive "enemy" (*SE* 327).

75. Following the humble Christ means moderating one's interior thoughts and feelings to avoid being a victim of anger or ego, and trying to explore alternative ways of dialogue and resolution. Tad Dunne, SJ, "Extremism in Ignatius of Loyola," *Review for Religious* 45, no. 3 (May–June 1986): 345–355.

76. Walking is one way to reflect on experience and find God (*SE* 77).

77. Joyce Rupp, *Walk in a Relaxed Manner: Life Lessons from the Camino* (Maryknoll, NY: Orbis Books, 2005).

78. This enigmatic phrase from Luke's Gospel sums up the personal nature of Ignatian prayer.

79. Joseph A. Munitiz, SJ, "St. Ignatius of Loyola and Severe Depression," *The Way* 44, no. 3 (July 2005): 69.

80. In times of desolation, people are led by the evil one, who guides and counsels falsely. They are tempted to give up on a positive outlook and adopt deceptive thoughts as their own (*SE* 318).

81. In the Principle and Foundation of Spiritual Exercise 23, Ignatius says that we must hold ourselves indifferent, or in balance, to be free to make wise and prudent choices.

82. The Sacred Heart of Jesus is an old devotion, dating from around the seventeenth century, about love for the heart of Jesus, the living, loving person of Christ. It is centered on the heart of Jesus as the symbol of divine love.

83. "Nothing can separate us from the love of God" (Romans 8:39) was proclaimed on Donal's memorial card.

84. Ignatius recommended removing yourself from distractions and noise to better hear God's voice (Annotation 20, *SE* 20).

85. Mark 15:34. In an extraordinary moment of humanity, Jesus quotes Psalm 22: "My God, my God, why have you forsaken me?"

86. Harold S. Kushner, *When Bad Things Happen to Good People* (New York: Anchor Books, 2004).

87. Sometimes prayer is not enough, and you have to do something concrete and challenging to break out of a rut (Paul Valadier, SJ, "Pray As If Everything Depends on You, Act As If Everything Depends on God," *Orientations for Spiritual Growth*, http://orientations.jesuits.ca/ hevenesi.pdf).

88. Console, a charity registered in Ireland that supports and helps people bereaved through suicide, offers support groups, counseling, and prevention programs (www.console.ie).

89. Good can come out of terrible grief or disasters, but God didn't intend or engineer these things to happen. The terrible pain of loss obscures any positive interpretation. See Richard Leonard, SJ, *Where the Hell Is God?* (Mahwah, NJ: Paulist Press, 2010).

90. It is impossible to know how many people have to drop out along the way, but anecdotally it seems a high percentage (see www.caminodesantiago.me/community/threads/dropout-rate.6799).

91. How we use something determines whether it brings us away from or closer to God. (David L. Fleming, SJ, *What Is Ignatian Spirituality?*

[Chicago: Loyola Press, 2008], 2–5.) See also
www.ignatianspirituality.com/ignatian-prayer/the-spiritualexercises/
ignatius-three-part-vision.

92. A key part of the *Spiritual Exercises* are the "Rules for Discernment" (*SE* 313–336), which encapsulate Ignatius's wisdom on dealing with moods and impulses. Some are so practical that I refer to them as rules of thumb. The one that applies here (318) is not to let changeable feelings dictate your actions; rather, stick to good decisions and sound rationales when making decisions (Michael O'Sullivan, SJ, "Trust Your Feelings but Use Your Head," *Studies in the Spirituality of Jesuits 22,* no. 4 [1990]: 21), (http://ejournals.bc.edu/ojs/index.php/jesuit/article/view/3910).

93. Mack, the central character in *The Shack,* uses this phrase to talk about his grief following the death of his beloved daughter, Missy, and about how he confronts God with his particular anger and resentment. This was something close to my own story that I could relate to (William Paul Young, *The Shack: Where Tragedy Confronts Eternity* [Los Angeles, CA: Windblown Media, 2007]).

94. This line echoes the words and structure that Ignatius used to describe one of his first spiritual insights, in which he uses reflection and interior examination to notice what's happening within him (Joseph N. Tylenda, SJ, *A Pilgrim's Journey* [Collegeville, MN: Liturgical Press, 1991], 14).

95. Mark Williams and Danny Penman, *Mindfulness: Finding Peace in a Frantic World* (New York: Rodale Books, 2011).

96. This is the essence of Anthony de Mello's teaching on awareness and "waking up" (www.demellospirituality.com/awareness/37.html).

97. Andy Otto, "The Ignatian Way: Contemplative in Action," *God in All Things,* (July 19, 2012), http://godinallthings.com/2012/07/19/the-ignatian-way-contemplative-in-action.

98. In Greek there are two words for time, *chronos* and *kairos. Chronos* refers to chronological or regimented "clock" time, while *kairos* means "out of time" or the "opportune time." It has a spiritual sense to it: time that is removed from the business of life, where the value of just being dominates.

99. Ignatius had a rule of thumb that when you are in doubt about someone's motives, it's helpful to begin with a positive interpretation of the person, to give him or her the benefit of the doubt (*SE* 22).

100. www.theway-themovie.com with Martin Sheen. I saw this as preparation before I left, but I didn't understand it until my return.

101. Steve Bevans, SVD, "God Is a Verb," *Catholic Theological Union* (October 2010), www.ctu.edu/word-ctu/article/god-verb

102. David Lonsdale, *Dance to the Music of the Spirit: The Art of Discernment* (London: Darton, Longman and Todd, 1992).

103. For example, Luke 24:36 and John 14:27.

104. The word *Eucharist* means "thanksgiving."

105. The paradox of a beauty that threatens, from William Butler Yeats's poem "Easter, 1916."

106. This same tension of being at the limits is evident in Jesus' statement on the cross, "My God, My God, why have you forsaken me?" (Matthew 27:46), which I often repeated to myself on the road.

107. The name of a Van Morrison song, meaning to face hardship, to take the hard road, not to have much choice.

108. Ignatius would call this the work of the destructive "bad spirit," planting doubts, lowering the mood, and raising obstacles to block progress (*SE* 315).

109. At 1,146 meters, El Palo is higher than any Irish mountain.

110. Gratitude is key to the Examen prayer, realizing how much we are loved.

111. This is a movement away from God and needs to be remedied by acting against it (*SE* 319).

112. Although the scale is obviously different in my brother's case, the examination of moods is still a valid subject matter for discernment (see Gerald O'Mahony, SJ, *Finding the Still Point* [Guildford, England: Eagle Publishing, 1992], 19–32).

113. Don't go back on good decisions when you made them in a free and balanced state (*SE* 318). See also Thomas H. Green, SJ, *Weeds among the Wheat* (Notre Dame, IN: Ave Maria Press, 1984), 107–111.

114. On a thirty-day pilgrimage across Spain in 1994, I had a similar crisis moment where, having run out of food, I realized I couldn't do it on my own and had to ask God to help me. That made all the difference.

115. Luke 23:46.

116. http://caminodesantiago.consumer.es/etapa-de-tineo-a-pola-de-allande (the 2011 app version).

117. Joseph Tetlow, SJ, *Ignatius Loyola: Spiritual Exercises* (New York: Crossroad, 1992), 54.

118. Walking the last 100 kilometers is the minimum requirement to get the official certificate, the *Compostela*.

119. Ignatius was very much a person of extremes in the early stages of his spiritual life at Manresa. At one point he even cut a hole in his shoes in order to suffer more while walking. Later he realized the folly of this and how much damage he had done to his health. He learned to be much more discerning, prudent, and balanced in decision making (Joseph N. Tylenda, SJ, chapter 3 in *A Pilgrim's Journey: The Autobiography of Ignatius of Loyola* [Collegeville, MN: Liturgical Press, 2001]).

120. Brendan McManus, SJ, "Surviving Suicide," *The Furrow* 61, no. 2 (February 2010).

121. I was grateful for this critical service. I needed to face up to the realities of what was coming up and, importantly, what my options were. It wasn't good enough just to drift along and stumble into choices; I needed to decide what my priorities were.

122. The image of an inner fire is central to Ignatius's idea of discernment: "Spiritual consolation is an experience of being so on fire with God's love"; "The soul comes to be inflamed with love of its Creator and Lord" (*SE* 316).

123. One refreshing thing about the Camino is that people rarely ask you about or define you in terms of your job or role; rather, it's about who you are and how you relate to others.

124. Matthew 5:5–8.

125. It was in the sense of being Nouwen's wounded healer that the trauma I had been through, far from being a block, could be of help for others. See Henri Nouwen, *The Wounded Healer: Ministry in Contemporary Society* (New York: Doubleday, 1972).

126. *SE* 319.

127. The Spanish name *Consuelo* is translated as "solace," "hope," or "consolation" and is linked to the Virgin Mary's title "Nuestra Señora del Consuelo," i.e., Our Lady of Consolation.

128. Michael Harter, SJ, ed., *Hearts on Fire: Praying with Jesuits* (Chicago: Loyola Press, 2005), 119.

129. James Martin, SJ. *The Jesuit Guide to (Almost) Everything* (New York: HarperOne, 2010), 264.

130. Reading Tolkien's *Lord of the Rings* as a teenager had made a deep impression on me, particularly in how the struggle for good over evil comes down to the deliberate actions of a few heroic individuals.

131. I felt I was called by this family and the situation to say a blessing. Being sensitive to the unexpected nature of God's call, I was just a humble instrument (*SE* 149–157).

132. Ignatius would probably call this desolation, and the little voice is the Spirit's call to right the unbalance (*SE* 317).

133. Alison Wertheimer, *A Special Scar: The Experiences of People Bereaved by Suicide*, 2nd ed. (Hove: Brunner-Routledge, 2001, second ed.), 77.

134. The restless unease, desolation, was indicating there was a problem with my highly individualistic plan and I needed to find a way to resolve it (*SE* 317).

135. Ignatius encourages us to ask for what we desire, to formulate our desire as prayer (*SE* 47–48).

136. This was a taste of what Jesus experienced in his passion and crucifixion (*SE* 203).

137. *The Breastplate of St. Patrick*, www.ourcatholicprayers.com/st-patricks-breastplate.html.

138. *Compostela* comes from the Latin *Campus Stellae* (i.e., Field of Stars). Legend has it that St. James's bones were carried from Jerusalem to northern Spain, where they were buried in a field in which a local shepherd later spotted a star. A church was built on this site, and it eventually became the famously beautiful Cathedral of Santiago de Compostela.

139. This was a remembering of all the gifts and graces I had received en route, and I was offering myself to God in the Liturgy of the Mass (*SE* 234).

140. The Eucharistic Prayer, or *Anaphora*, is the central part of the Mass, which contains the prayer of thanksgiving and the consecration of the bread and wine.

141. At that particular time they were using the old translation of Eucharistic Prayer II. The new translation (2011) reads well too: "Remember also our brothers and sisters who have fallen asleep in the hope of the Resurrection and all who have died in your mercy: welcome them into the light of your face."

142. Ignatius asks us in the Third Week of the Exercises to personalize our connection with Jesus, feeling tears and grief for what he has suffered for us (*SE* 203).

143. I was deeply affected by the debate over suicide and hell. See Brendan McManus, SJ, "Surviving Suicide," *The Furrow* 61, no. 2 (February 2010).

144. David L. Fleming, SJ, "Prayer Is a Conversation," *What Is Ignatian Spirituality?* www.ignatianspirituality.com/ignatian-prayer/the-spiritual-exercises/prayer-is-a-conversation.

145. Discernment for Ignatius meant examining our interior movements, or moods, and observing whether they lead in a good or bad direction (David L. Fleming, SJ, *Draw Me into Your Friendship—The Spiritual Exercises: A Literal Translation and a Contemporary Reading* [St. Louis: Institute of Jesuit Resources, 1996], 243–245).

146. *SE* 313–336.

147. This is another example of *agere contra*, acting against the instinct for inertia or stagnation and opening up to new possibilities (*SE* 13).

148. William Johnston, ed., *The Cloud of Unknowing and the Book of Privy Counseling* (New York: Doubleday, 1973).

149. This is a definition of consolation, an inner movement that comes from God (*SE* 316).

150. Ignatius, in his note on doing penance, seeks to have the external act mirror the internal desire of asking God for some special favor or grace (*SE* 87). By doing penance here, I brought my whole body into the act

of asking God for release from this burden of grief. I committed myself fully to the prayer and the process, psychologically and now physically, in underlying my desire for God's grace.

151. Don't undo a good decision just because you experience doubts or resistance (*SE* 319).

152. Ignatius would have called this deep consolation, being on fire with God's love and realizing that everything is a freely given gift, a "fourth week" experience (*SE* 234).

153. Joseph N. Tylenda, SJ, *A Pilgrim's Journey: The Autobiography of Ignatius of Loyola* (Collegeville, MN: Liturgical Press, 2001), 31. See also Brian O'Leary, "What New Life Is This?" *Irish Messenger* (December 2006), www.catholicireland.net/what-new-life-is-this/.

# Select References and Recommended Further Reading

Aschenbrenner, George, SJ. "Consciousness Examen." *Review for Religious* 31, no. 1 (January 1972): 14–21.

Barry, William A. "Discernment: How Do I Know I'm Experiencing God?" www.ignatianspirituality.com/making-good-decisions/discernment-of-spirits/how-do-i-know-im-experiencing-god.

de Mello Spirituality Center, www.demellospirituality.com.

Dunne, Tad. "Extremism in Ignatius of Loyola." *Review for Religious* 45, no. 3 (May–June 1986): 345–355.

English, John J. *Spiritual Freedom: From an Experience of the Ignatian Exercises to the Art of Spiritual Guidance.* 2nd ed. Chicago: Loyola Press, 1995.

Estevez, Emilio, Jack Hitt. *The Way.* Directed by Emilio Estevez. Barcelona, Spain: Filmax Entertainment, October 2011. www.theway-themovie.com.

Federación Española de Asociaciones de Amigos del Camino de Santiago. www.caminosantiago.org/cpperegrino/comun/inicio.asp.

Fleming, David L. *Draw Me into Your Friendship—The Spiritual Exercises: A Literal Translation and a Contemporary Reading.* St. Louis: Institute of Jesuit Sources, 1996.

Green, Thomas H. *Weeds among the Wheat.* Notre Dame, IN: Ave Maria Press, 1984.

Grogan, Brian. *Alone and on Foot: Ignatius of Loyola.* Dublin: Veritas, 2009.

Harter, Michael, ed. *Hearts on Fire: Praying with Jesuits*. Chicago: Loyola Press, 2005.

Hughes, Gerard W. *In Search of a Way: Two Journeys of Spiritual Discovery*. London: Darton, Longman and Todd, 1986.

Ignatian Camino. http://caminoignaciano.org/en.

Ignatian Spirituality. www.ignatianspirituality.com.

Ivens, Michael. *An Approach to Saint Ignatius of Loyola*. Edited by Joseph Munitiz. Oxford: Way Books, 2008.

Kushner, Harold S. *When Bad Things Happen to Good People*. New York: Anchor Books, 2004.

Lehane, Brian J. "Attitude of Gratitude: The Examen Prayer of St. Ignatius." *Partners*. www.jesuits-chgdet.org/wp-content/uploads/011/03/Partners_FA09.Sprituality.pdf.

Leonard, Richard. *Where the Hell Is God?* Mahwah, NJ: Paulist Press, 2010.

Lonsdale, David. *Dance to the Music of the Spirit: The Art of Discernment*. London: Darton, Longman and Todd, 1992.

Lowney, Chris. *Heroic Leadership*. Chicago: Loyola Press, 2003.

Martin, James, SJ. *The Jesuit Guide to (Almost) Everything*. New York: HarperOne, 2010.

McManus, Brendan, SJ. "Surviving Suicide." *The Furrow* 61, no. 2 (February 2010).

McManus, Brendan, SJ. "Ignatian Pilgrimage: The Inner Journey—Loyola to Manresa on Foot." *The Way* 9, no. 3 (July 2010).

Muller, Peter, and Angel Fernandez de Aranguiz. *Every Pilgrim's Guide to Walking to Santiago de Compostela*. Translated by Laurie Dennett. Norwich: Canterbury Press, 2010.

Munitiz, Joseph. "St. Ignatius of Loyola and Severe Depression." *The Way* 44, no. 3 (July 2005): 58–59.

O'Leary, Brian. *Ignatian Spirituality*. Dublin: Messenger Publications, 2009.

O'Mahony, Gerald. *Finding the Still Point*. Guilford, England: Eagle Publishing, 1992.

O'Sullivan, Michael. "Trust Your Feelings, but Use Your Head." *Studies in the Spirituality of Jesuits* 22, no. 4 (1990).

Otto, Andy. "The Ignatian Way: Contemplative in Action." *God in All Things*. (July 19, 2012). http://godinallthings.com/2012/07/19/the-ignatian-way-contemplative-in-action.

Pope Francis. *The Joy of the Gospel: Evangelii Gaudium*. Frederick, MD: Word among Us Press, 2014.

Rohr, Richard. *Falling Upward: A Spirituality for the Two Halves of Life*. London: Society for Promoting Christian Knowledge, 2011.

Rupp, Joyce. *Praying Our Goodbyes: A Spiritual Companion through Life's Losses and Sorrows*. Notre Dame, IN: Ave Maria Press, 1988.

Rupp, Joyce. *Walk in a Relaxed Manner: Life Lessons from the Camino*. Maryknoll, NY: Orbis Books, 2005.

Silf, Margaret. *Inner Compass: An Invitation to Ignatian Spirituality*. Chicago: Loyola Press, 1998.

Tylenda, Joseph N. *A Pilgrim's Journey: The Autobiography of Ignatius of Loyola*. Collegeville, MN: Liturgical Press, 1991.

URCamino, Camino de Santiago information, www.urcamino.com.

Veale, Joseph. "The Dynamic of the Exercises." *The Way*, Supplement, 52 (Spring 1985).

Wertheimer, Alison. *A Special Scar: The Experiences of People Bereaved by Suicide*. 2nd ed. Hove: Brunner-Routledge, 2001.

Williams, Mark, and Danny Penman. *Mindfulness: Finding Peace in a Frantic World*. New York: Rodale Books, 2011.

Williams, Monty. *The Gift of Spiritual Intimacy: Following the Spiritual Exercises of Saint Ignatius*. Toronto, ON: Novalis, 2009.

*Note: Reading the* Spiritual Exercises *of St. Ignatius directly is a frustrating affair as they are originally written as guidelines for retreat directors who have to adapt them to persons and contexts as needed; hence they seem turgid and obscure for many readers. Instead, I suggest some of the excellent guides to and interpretations of the* Spiritual Exercises, *such as the Fleming, O'Leary, and Silf books listed above.*

# A Ritual for Bereavement

Based on the Camino experience, this is a suggested list of steps for someone working through a loss. Ideally, this process would be facilitated by a spiritual guide, director, or soul friend (*anam cara*).

1. Get in touch with your deepest desire. What is it you really want at this stage in your bereavement process? To do this means to place yourself in the hands of God, explicitly admitting that a solution is beyond yourself.

2. Present yourself to God in a prayer asking for the healing or grace you want, but be open to what God wants for you; e.g., *Give me some peace of mind with this terrible grief, but not my will but yours be done.*

3. Select a symbol of the person whom you have lost, something that evokes him or her strongly, such as a piece of clothing, a photo, or a personal item.

4. Give yourself a physical challenge that will stretch you—not one that's impossible, but one that has some ascetic quality and some meditative element. Carry your symbol with you on this challenge. For example, walk to a special place, climb a mountain, swim a certain number of lengths in a pool, or cycle a route that is special for you.

5. Prepare a ritual that has meaning for you; e.g., burning a piece of the person's clothing, burying a journal of your grief, refurbishing a favorite chair of your beloved, prayerfully disposing of his or her personal effects, or honoring a special photo.

6. Afterward, do a simple purification with water, like having a long shower, a dip in a pool, or a swim in the sea. Remember your birth in the Spirit (i.e., baptism) and how you are a child of God, renewed by Christ.

7. Finally, reflect on the whole process to see where you have been moved, if there is a new freedom in you or not, or simply where God has been present. Write up your reflections in a private journal. You may have to repeat this process a number of times, adjusting certain elements as you go. Notice where you might be getting stuck, and pray for help with that part.

# Ignatius of Loyola's Guidelines for Negotiating Life's Journey

1. Remember that you are a pilgrim, just passing through life. You put yourself on the road, a journey into the unknown, to be open to hear God's call.
2. God is a pilgrim who's always trying to find us, even in difficult situations. God is with you even if you are not with God.
3. Walking puts you in touch with your deeper desires, what you really want. Following this longing will bring us to God.
4. Keep on track by following the signs that are found only in reflection and meditation. Trust your inner compass to guide you.
5. Take time out regularly to reflect on your path (i.e., Review of the Day); be flexible in progressively altering things as you go. Don't be afraid of change.
6. Take time over decisions; they are important "crossroads" moments in your life. Never make a hasty decision—rather, play for time, and ponder the options internally before deciding.

7. If you get lost, be humble enough to backtrack to a known, sure spot. Beware of pride driving you on, getting you even more lost.

8. Possessions are only temporary; don't hold on to things too tightly. Practice detachment: use things insofar as they are useful, and discard them when they get in the way.

9. You can expect fierce storms on the road. The important thing is not to be deterred from your course but to hang on tightly to those support structures you know to be sound (prayer, discernment, and reflection). Don't change course, undo decisions, or alter the structure in midstorm.

10. Protecting yourself is important, as is having good defenses against whatever comes. This means knowing your own weak spots and "unfree" areas, as this is where you are likely to be vulnerable. (Ignatius recommends fortifying your defenses to anticipate challenges.)

# About the Author

Brendan McManus's love of the outdoors comes from being raised on a farm in Northern Ireland. After studying psychology and information technology at Ulster University, he worked in the UK's computer industry as an interface designer. Disillusioned with the "yuppie" way of life, Brendan left to join the Jesuits in Dublin. As a Jesuit student, he worked with young people, leading retreats and pilgrimages. Later, as a priest, he worked with the Gardiner Street Gospel Choir in Dublin and developed his writing skills as editor of the *Irish Jesuit News*. A keen hiker, Brendan's love of pilgrimage emerged during his Jesuit training when he and a companion begged their way across northern Spain. He was a school chaplain and photographer in Coláiste Iognáid, Galway, before walking the Camino in 2011. He currently works in spiritual direction, and writes and offers retreats in Belfast. Learn more about Brendan and his journey at redemptionroadcamino.com.

# Other Books by Jesuit Authors

### Reimagining the Ignatian Examen
*Fresh Ways to Pray from Your Day*

MARK E. THIBODEAUX, SJ
Paperback | 4244-1 | $9.95

### A Purposeful Path
*How Far Can You Go with $30,
a Bus Ticket, and a Dream?*

CASEY BEAUMIER, SJ
Paperback | 4250-2 | $13.95

### What's So Funny About Faith?
*A Memoir from the Intersection of
Hilarious and Holy*

JAKE MARTIN, SJ
Paperback | 3739-3 | $13.95

### My Life with the Saints

JAMES MARTIN, SJ
Paperback | 2644-1 | $15.95

# Also Available

## Rock-Bottom Blessings
*Discovering God's Abundance When All Seems Lost*

KAREN BEATTIE
Paperback | 3842-0 | $13.95

## The Thorny Grace of It
*And Other Essays for Imperfect Catholics*

BRIAN DOYLE
Paperback | 3906-9 | $14.95

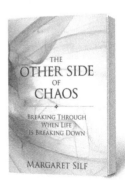

## The Other Side of Chaos
*Breaking Through When Life is Breaking Down*

MARGARET SILF
Paperback | 3308-1 | $13.95

# Continue the Conversation
## www.LoyolaPress.com

If you enjoyed this book, then connect with Loyola Press to continue the conversation, engage with other readers, and find out about new and upcoming books from your favorite spiritual writers. Visit us at **www.LoyolaPress.com** to create an account and register for our newsletters. Or scan the code below with your smartphone.

Connect with us through:

 **Facebook**
facebook.com
/loyolapress

 **Twitter**
twitter.com
/loyolapress

 **YouTube**
youtube.com
/loyolapress